ENGLISH **PANORAMA** 1

A course for advanced learners

STUDENT'S BOOK

Felicity O'Dell

CAMBRIDGE
UNIVERSITY PRESS

PUBLISHED BY THE PRESS SYNDICATE OF THE UNIVERSITY OF CAMBRIDGE
The Pitt Building, Trumpington Street, Cambridge, United Kingdom

CAMBRIDGE UNIVERSITY PRESS
The Edinburgh Building, Cambridge CB2 2RU, UK   http://www.cup.cam.ac.uk
40 West 20th Street, New York, NY 10011–4211, USA   http://www.cup.org
10 Stamford Road, Oakleigh, Melbourne 3166, Australia

First published 1997
Reprinted 1999

Printed in the United Kingdom at the University Press, Cambridge

ISBN 0 521 47687 9 Student's Book
ISBN 0 521 47688 7 Teacher's Book
ISBN 0 521 47689 5 Set of 2 cassettes

Contents

Map of the book		4
1	Snow White – or wicked stepmother?	6
2	Here is the news!	13
3	Look it up!	19
4	So deliciously tempting	26
5	As the saying goes	31
6	Chasing dreams	36
7	Deluged with information	42
8	Amusing in retrospect	50
9	Gifts from the boss	58
10	I can't agree with you!	65
11	People might have been happier then	72
12	Game, set and match	81
13	Shoot with care	90
14	Thank you for calling	97
15	Six Dinner Sid	104
16	Let's take a closer look	110
17	Dear Sir or Madam	116
18	Making small talk	123
19	We're talking epic here	129
20	Verbal hygiene for women	137
21	Love is blind	143
22	Killing a cad	149
23	A twilight area	154
24	Yes, Prime Minister	163
Tapescripts		168
Phonetic symbols		175
Acknowledgements		176

Unit		Reading/listening	Speaking/writing
1	Snow White – or wicked stepmother?	Reading – Biography	Writing – A CV
2	Here is the news	Listening – News broadcast	Speaking – The IPA
3	Look it up!	Reading – Language reference books	Speaking – Stress in words and sentences
4	So deliciously tempting	Listening – Radio adverts	Writing – Error correction
5	As the saying goes	Reading – Sayings	Writing – A proverb story
6	Chasing dreams	Listening – Songs	Speaking – Rhyme
7	Deluged with information	Reading – A mail order catalogue	Writing – Planning and writing a discursive essay
8	Amusing in retrospect	Listening – Anecdotes	Speaking – Expressing interest
9	Gifts from the boss	Reading – Business articles	Speaking – Weak forms
10	I can't agree with you!	Listening – Giving opinions	Speaking – Giving a talk
11	People might have been happier then	Reading – Magazine articles	Writing – Reports
12	Game, set and match	Listening – Sports reports	Writing – Being accurate
13	Shoot with care	Reading – Instructions	Speaking – Intonation
14	Thank you for calling	Listening – Telephone messages	Writing – Notes and messages
15	Six Dinner Sid	Reading – Children's stories	Speaking – Reading aloud
16	Let's take a closer look	Listening – Tourist guides	Writing – Taking notes
17	Dear Sir or Madam	Reading – Letters	Writing – Punctuation
18	Making small talk	Listening – Snippets of conversation	Speaking – Making small talk
19	We're talking epic here	Reading – Reviews	Speaking – Criticising tactfully
20	Verbal hygiene for women	Listening – Lecture	Speaking – Pronunciation of consonant groups
21	Love is blind	Reading – Scientific article	Writing – Summaries
22	Killing a cad	Listening – Short story	Writing – Beginnings and endings
23	A twilight area	Reading – Drama	Speaking – Expressing feeling when you speak
24	Yes, Prime Minister	Listening – Comedy	Writing – Addressing your readers

Grammar	Vocabulary	Study skills
Assessing your strengths and weaknesses	Ways of writing down vocabulary	Recording your current level of English
The grammar of news reporting	Learning words in groups	Listening to the news at home
Prepositions	Collocations	
Adverbials expressing attitude	Positive and negative words	Keeping your ears and eyes open
Gerunds	Vocabulary of sayings	
Non-standard English	Affixes	Learning from songs
Infinitives	Words from the same root	
Past tenses	Phrasal verbs	Improving your reading speed
Singular and plural	Business English	Collecting and using articles
Questions and answers	Discourse markers	
Modals	Register	
More modals	Idioms	Assessing progress
Structures with particular verbs	Spelling	English and your own language
Variations on standard patterns of reported speech	Euphemisms and political correctness	
Unusual conditionals	Collocations	Making your own exercises
Prepositions	Homophones	
Perfect forms of the verb	Vocabulary from the texts	Problem-solving
Pronunciation	Compound nouns	
Complex sentences	Topic vocabulary	What to read in English
Continuous forms of the verb	Words and their associations	
Expressing concepts in science	Tautologies	Checking your reading speed
Ellipsis	Slang	
Nuances of meaning	Adverbs of manner	Speaking with a text
Countables and uncountables	Ambiguity	Looking back and forwards

Snow White – or wicked stepmother? *Biography*

The main
aspects of
language
worked on in
this unit are:

- reading and writing a biographical article
- ways of writing down new vocabulary
- writing a curriculum vitae
- a grammar test to assess your strengths and weaknesses
- recording your level of English at this point

Warm-up: Getting to know people

1 Take a blank card or half a sheet of paper. Note down on the
card the things suggested below.

Three things you're good at
Three things you're not good at
Three famous people (living or dead) whom you'd like to invite to dinner
Three words to describe the place where you were born
Three places where you like to be

2 Now mix with other
students in the class. Show
each other your pieces of
paper. Ask each other
questions to find out more
about anything you have
written.

Reading: Biographical article

1 Work in pairs. Discuss the following questions.

a How much do you know about Walt Disney? His work? His life?
His character?

b If you don't know much about his life or character, could you
make any predictions based on what you know about his work?

2 Read the text, which comes
from *The Observer*, a British
Sunday newspaper. In pairs
note down the facts in it
about Walt Disney's work,
life and character.

Not so Snow White after all

Walter Elias Disney Jr, officially born 1901 in Chicago (though possibly ten years earlier in the Spanish town of Mojacar) is arguably one of the greatest artists of all time. A legend in his lifetime, Disney shaped fairy tales into compelling new patterns, and while fighting off creditors, took immense financial risks as he innovated, experimented and went out on limbs, always refusing to cut corners for profit.

Disney was not a graphic artist of great skill. The famous scrolled signature that became the company's logo had to be taught to him by an employee, and in 1920 he was laid off by a Kansas City advertising company with a comment on his 'singular lack of drawing ability'. But he had a gift for assembling creative teams and great ambition. He knew what he wanted and could see when things were going wrong; even though he was not always capable of articulating his thoughts, he could act out a whole movie that he carried in his head, so that his animators could see it before them.

In 1920 he made the first sound cartoon (much influenced by his hero, Charlie Chaplin, who inspired Mickey Mouse). He was the first film-maker to see the appeal of Technicolor and to move entirely into colour film. In 1934, at the height of the Depression, he increased his staff to 1,500 so he could embark on a seemingly foolhardy programme of feature-length cartoons, and over the next eight years made *Snow White*, *Pinocchio*, *Fantasia*, *Dumbo* and *Bambi*, films that remain unsurpassed for imaginative soundtrack, for which cinemas were not yet ready.

In the mid 1950s, as other studios dithered, Disney struck a deal with the ABC television network for a weekly peaktime series which for the first time eased his cash-flow problems. As its avuncular presenter, Disney's face became as famous as his name. At the same time he conceived Disneyland, and two years later, after a comically disastrous opening day, the turnstiles of the world's first theme park were happily clicking away. Shortly before his death he created in Cal-Arts a university.

The artistic achievement, public adulation and financial success brought neither satisfaction nor happiness. Disney was a sad, depressed, remote figure, a poor father, an inconsiderate husband, a three-pack-a-day smoker and near-alcoholic who disapproved of drinking. He regarded his employees as a family, but paid them badly and stole their credits, treated them as traitors (and branded them as Communist subversives) if they opposed him. No Jew made it into his executive ranks, no woman got a better job than as a lowly colourer, the only black employed in his studio was a veteran shoeshine boy. It has also been established that from 1940 Disney was an informer for the FBI and had a role in attracting the House Un-American Activities Committee to investigate Tinseltown's politics.

The FBI association was connected with Disney's fears over his parentage that began with his discovery that his birth had never been registered. In return for Walt informing on his colleagues, J. Edgar Hoover apparently undertook to trace his origins. This trail led him to an attractive washerwoman called Isabella Zamora Ascensio in late 19th-century Spain. Three American teams visited her home town, Almeria, the first in 1940, the last in 1967 just after Walt's death. What they discovered is a mystery, though it seems likely that the 1967 party was bent on destroying evidence rather than finding anything out.

---

3 This article is partly based on the contrast between what one might expect a popular maker of films and theme parks for children to be like as a person and what Walt Disney was really like. What points of contrast does the article make?

4 Write a heading for each of the paragraphs in the text. For example, a heading for the first paragraph could be *Disney's achievements in brief*.

Vocabulary: Ways of writing down new vocabulary

Do you have a special notebook or a special section in your file where you write down new words and expressions that you want to learn? These exercises are about how to make use of this notebook or section of your file in ways that will be most helpful for you.

1 Follow these instructions.

1 Read through the Walt Disney text again and underline in pencil all the words and expressions whose meaning you do not know (or did not know before reading the article).
2 Ask your teacher or use a dictionary to find out the meaning of these words and expressions.
3 Now look again at the words and expressions you underlined. Some of them are likely to seem much more useful to you than others. Which of them do you particularly want to learn?

2 Answer these questions.

a What are the different ways in which you can write things down in your vocabulary notebook? Take the word *innovation*, for example. How many different ways can you think of for writing it down if you wanted to learn it? Here are two suggestions to start you off: *innovation* + translation, *innovation* and other words from the same family like *to innovate* and *innovative*.
b Your teacher has at least ten ideas for ways of writing it down. How many of these did you think of?
c Some of these ways of writing words down are particularly suitable for particular sorts of words and expressions. Which ways do you think would be especially appropriate for the following words and expressions?
wicked; stepmother; dwarf; was laid off; feature-length; cartoon; FBI; bent on

3 Work with a partner and follow these instructions.

1 Look at some of the words and expressions from the article that you both decided you would like to learn.
2 Discuss which techniques you would want to use when writing down these words and expressions in your vocabulary notebook.
3 Write those words and expressions down in the ways you discussed.

Writing: A CV

Writing a biographical article (like the one on Walt Disney), the writer:

a looks back over his or her subject's life;

b summarises the most important strands in that life;

c normally attempts to show both the good and the bad aspects of a person's life;

d gives his or her own personal opinions about the subject's life;

e tries to use language in an effective way with the aim of catching and holding the reader's interest;

f has considerable freedom in the style and format used.

A CV (curriculum vitae), referred to in American English as a résumé, is a piece of paper written by someone who is applying for a job, giving basic information about his or her life.

1 Discuss these questions with a partner.

a Which of the points a to f above apply to a CV as well as to a biographical article?

b Why are the other characteristics of a biographical article not appropriate for a CV?

2 Here is an example of a CV, written in the style used in the UK. Answer these questions.

a What kind of position do you think this person would be suitable for?

b Whose CV do you think it is?

Name:	???
Date of birth:	14th November 1948
Nationality:	British
Marital status:	Divorced. Two sons.
Professional experience:	1976– Voluntary charity work 1971–76 Royal Navy
Education:	1970 Graduated in archaeology, anthropology and history (Cantab) 1966 Geelong Grammar School, Australia 1961–1966 Gordonstoun School, Scotland
Languages spoken:	English, French, Welsh
Publications:	*The Old Man of Lochnagar* (a children's story) *A Vision of Britain* (an essay on architecture)
Leisure interests:	Polo, sketching, fox hunting, gardening, travelling

3 Look at the CV in Exercise 2 again and answer these questions.

a Some of the headings used in the example CV would need to be used by any candidate applying for any job, and some are appropriate only for some people and/or some jobs. Which headings are appropriate in all circumstances and which only in some situations?

b Can you think of any other headings which might be useful in a CV?

c For what kind of jobs might it be appropriate to use headings like *marital status*, *languages spoken* and any other headings that are not required in all circumstances?

d What should applicants put first when presenting different elements of their professional experience and their education in a CV?

e Is it better for a CV to be long or short?

4 Now prepare your own CV by following these instructions.

1 Choose a job that you would be interested in applying for.
2 Discuss with a partner what kind of information (a) you personally would give about yourself in a CV applying for any job you might be interested in and (b) you would include in an application for the specific job you have in mind.
3 Write your CV for that job.

4 Give your CV to your partner and ask for comments on it. Is everything clear? Do you seem to have missed out anything important? Can your partner see any mistakes in your English?
5 If necessary, make changes before handing it to your teacher for any corrections and further comments.

Grammar: Diagnostic test

Do these exercises on your own without asking for help or using any reference materials. Having corrected them, your teacher will then tell you which areas you need to do some extra work on.

1 Do you need *a(n)*, *the* or – in each of the gaps in this text? Write the correct one in each gap.

One of my old friends from (1) .... university now works as (2) .... long-distance lorry driver. Although she spent five years studying (3) .... art history and even wrote (4) .... dissertation on (5) .... art of (6) .... Renaissance in (7) .... Italy, she has no regrets about abandoning (8) .... academic career and taking up (9) .... very different kind of (10) .... work. She often travels to (11) .... foreign countries and thinks nothing of going on (12) .... European journey which involves crossing (13) .... Alps all on her own.

2 Fill in the correct preposition in each of the gaps in the text below.

The man walked quietly (1) .... the counter (2) .... the end (3) .... the bank. He then pulled a gun (4) .... his pocket and pointed it (5) .... the cashier. She burst (6) .... tears, saying, 'It's my first day here and it's my birthday.' The man paused (7) .... a moment, giving her time to throw herself (8) .... the ground and to press the alarm bell. The police arrived (9) .... the bank (10) .... minutes and charged the man (11) .... attempted robbery (12) .... violence.

3 Choose the correct form of the verbs in brackets to complete each text.

When we (1) .... (enter) the station, lots of people (2) .... (stand) on the platform (3) .... (wait) for the train. Eventually, the station master (4) .... (make) an announcement over the loudspeaker. The train (5) .... (delay) by flooding on the line and (6) .... (only just leave) Manchester. It (7) .... (not arrive) for another hour.

By this time next year I (8) .... (leave) school. I (9) .... (do) my final school exams in December and (10) .... (definitely not go) back to school in January. I (11) .... (think) I (12) .... (probably be able) (13) .... (find) some work in a café while I (14) .... (wait) for my results. If I (15) .... (pass) all my exams, I (16) .... (go) to university in September. I (17) .... (let) you know as soon as I (18) .... (get) the results. I (19) .... (wish) now that I (20) .... (work) harder at school. I (21) .... (have) more chance of getting good marks in my exams.

4 Are the sentences below correct or not? If they contain an error, correct them.

a Please could you give me an advice. I'd like some informations about accommodations in your country.

b She's looking for a new work. She has an interview tomorrow for the job of manager in a shop selling furnitures. But I think with her beautiful long black hairs she should be a model.

c Could I have a fruit, please. And a bread and some cheese too. That'll do for my lunch.

5 Match the function in the list on the right with the appropriate sentence, a–h.

a You might be right.
b You should have your hair cut.
c You must have your hair cut at once.
d You may swim if you wish.
e You shall go to the ball, Cinderella.
f The phone's ringing. I'll answer it.
g The train must have been delayed.
h Won't you sit down, please.

Permission
Promise
Deduction
Possibility
Advice
Invitation
Offer
Order

6 Rewrite each sentence using the verb at the beginning of the line in an appropriate form. What you write should be as close as possible to the meaning of the original sentence.

a 'Jack, you stole my bike,' said Jane.
   accuse ....
b Most parents would be happy if their children found good jobs.
   want ....
c Do you mind if I open the window?
   object ....
d I don't think you are right.
   agree ....
e You mustn't eat in the classrooms.
   allow ....
f Your boss can force you to wear a uniform if she wants to.
   make ....
g The police think his wife killed him.
   suspect ....
h 'I'm sorry I embarrassed you, Mary,' said Dick.
   apologise ....
i I wish I had a home like hers.
   envy ....
j Put down your pens now, please.
   stop ....

Study skills: Recording your level of English now

At this level it can be difficult to appreciate just how much progress you make with your English. The exercises below are to encourage you to make a record of both your spoken and your written English at the beginning of this new course. Keep the record, and at the end of the course you will be able to compare your work then with how it is now.

1 The journalist who wrote about Walt Disney could have written a straight biographical account of his life similar to something you might find in an encyclopedia, but he managed to make it more interesting by using some techniques typical of articles written about people.

Which of these typical techniques did the writer of the Walt Disney article use?

a an interesting title
b making comments as well as stating facts
c highlighting contrasts
d referring to physical appearance
e using occasional direct speech
f talking about feelings as well as facts
g giving specific examples rather than just making generalisations
h mentioning something mysterious or unusual

2 An important part of writing an interesting article about someone is asking the right questions in your initial interview. Clearly, open and possibly unusual questions are likely to receive more productive answers than yes/no or very standard questions.

⌨ Listen to the tape and write down the questions. Now discuss the following with a partner.

a Which questions do you think would and which would not be helpful for a journalist?

b If you did not find some of the questions very satisfactory, how could they be improved?

As a class, discuss some other questions which could be useful when interviewing a subject for an article.

3 Work with a partner. Take it in turns to interview each other using some of the questions discussed in the previous activity, but adding any more that occur to you as the interview progresses. You may want to take notes as you conduct your interview.

Record your interviews on an audio cassette. Keep the recordings in a safe place.

4 Write a short biographical article based on your interview. Use as many as possible of the techniques listed in Exercise 1 – and any others which will help to make your article effective. After your teacher has corrected your article, keep it in a safe place.

Here is the news
Radio news

The main aspects of language worked on in this unit are:	• listening to news broadcasts • the International Phonetic Alphabet • the grammar of news reporting • learning words in groups • listening to the news in English at home

Warm-up: The news

Answer these questions.

a How often do you listen to or watch the news?
b What sorts of stories usually make the news?
c Does the news differ from one country to another? If so, in what ways?

Soapstar in courtroom drama

Prince to divorce

MP admits taking £50,000

Footballers strip bungle

PM's cat does runner

Schoolgirl bride has popstar's baby

Better burgers scandal

OAPs revolt

Pope to visit Las Vegas

Internet going cheap to schools

Inflation soars

Listening: News broadcast

1 Listen to the news broadcast and write brief notes about each of the stories in the table below.

Story	Where?	When?	What?	Who?
1				
2				
3				
4				

2 Work with a partner.

1 Compare what you wrote in the table with your partner.
2 How much extra information can you remember about each of the four items?
3 Listen again to each item in the broadcast to check the information that you remembered and to add any further information.

Grammar: News reporting

1 ▭ Below are some sentences from each of the four items in the broadcast. In each case some verbs are missing. Can you complete the gaps with the correct forms of the necessary verbs? The verbs which you will need for the first two sets of sentences can all be found in the boxes below, but for the final sets, you are on your own. Listen to the tape again and check or complete your answers.

Item 1

a At least 45 people .... (now) .... in the California earthquake. The US President .... the area today .... for himself the scene of the devastation. It .... the worst earthquake that the country .... for over three decades. Thousands of residents .... a second night camped out in parks and gardens.

b As aftershocks .... on, the shock .... in.

c But only one in five of the local population .... against earthquakes and so thousands of people .... everything.

be	die	insure	know	lose	rumble
see	sink	spend	suffer	visit	

Item 2

a Figures out today .... that retail sales last year ....worse than ....

b And there .... a sharp rise in inflation.

be	expect	show

Item 3

English Aerospace .... a further 400 jobs at their Birmingham and Manchester plants. Last week they .... that 75 workers in Liverpool .... their jobs.

Item 4

Crime figures released today .... that illegal drugs worth more than £500 billion .... by Customs and Excise last year. Record hauls of cocaine and amphetamines .... Customs officers .... in .... up a number of drug rings and over 100 arrests ....

2 Now discuss these questions about the grammar of the verb forms used with other students in your class.

a Which form is used twice above to talk about the future? Do you think this form is commonly used in other contexts?

b How often is the present perfect used? Does this seem to be relatively frequent usage of the present perfect to you? Why do you think the present perfect is (or is not) used relatively frequently in news reporting?

c How often is the passive used in the extracts from these items above? Why is the passive relatively common in news broadcasts?

d In the first item above, what forms are *rumble* and *sink* in? Could these forms be reversed (the *rumble* form used with *sink* and vice versa)? If so, what effect would this have?

3 Follow these instructions.

1 Listen to a recorded version of yesterday's or today's news in English. Note down any examples of *are to do*, the present perfect and the passive. Also note whether any present tenses are in the simple or the continuous form. In each case explain why this form is used.

2 Find a newspaper article reporting on a story currently in the news, perhaps one about one of the stories from the broadcast you listened to.

3 Write a brief summary of the content of the article. Make sure your summary covers the basic questions Where? When? What? and Who? and includes any other information of particular importance.

4 Note whether the use of verb forms reflects what you noticed about the use of verb forms in news broadcasts in Exercise 2.

5 Compare articles and comments on the language they use with other students.

Speaking: Pronunciation and the IPA

1 English pronunciation is famous for being difficult – in that the spelling can often be confusing. How many different ways can you find for pronouncing the letters *o*, *a* and *ea* in just the short news broadcast you listened to at the beginning of this unit? Look at the tapescript on page 168. Note down words which illustrate each of the different sounds for each letter or pair of letters. You should find at least five different pronunciations in each case.

o ....

a ....

ea ....

Fortunately, good dictionaries use an international phonetic alphabet which tells you how words are pronounced. Most of the consonants in the phonetic alphabet are easy to learn as they are the same as the ordinary English letters. The only ones which you need to learn specially are /ʃ/ (sh), /ʒ/ (s as in *treasure*), /θ/ (th in *thin*), /ð/ (th in *then*) and /ŋ/ (ng). You will find a key to the phonetic alphabet in any dictionary which uses it and in this book on page 175.

The vowels are more difficult and are especially useful to learn because, as we have seen, they are particularly illogical in their pronunciation.

2 Look at the symbols for the vowels below and follow these instructions.

1 🔊 Listen to the tape and write the words you hear in the correct place in the third column.

2 Add one more example to the remaining rows in the third column.

Symbol	Example words	More examples
/ɑː/	start, last, after	
/æ/	act, back, happen	
/aɪ/	wife, cry	
/aɪə/	fire, tyre	
/aʊ/	out, loud	
/aʊə/	flour, tower	
/e/	met, head, pen	
/eɪ/	say, face, break	
/eə/	fair, care, wear	
/ɪ/	win, list, pit	
/iː/	me, feed, reason	
/ɪə/	year, beard, area	
/ɒ/	drop, pot, gone	
/əʊ/	note, phone, total	
/ɔː/	more, lord, saw	
/ɔɪ/	boy, coin, point	
/ʊ/	would, stood	
/uː/	you, lose, choose	
/ʊə/	sure, pure, cure	
/ɜː/	turn, third, earth	
/ʌ/	cut, one, must, company	
/ə/	butter, total, against	

3 Translate the parts of the text which are in the IPA into ordinary English spelling.

A man was walking in the park and came across a penguin. hi tʊk hɪm tuː ə pəliːsmən ənd sed, 'aɪv faʊnd ðɪs peŋgwɪn, wɒt ʃəd aɪ duː?' ðə pəliːsmən aːnsəd, 'teɪk hɪm tuː ðə zuː.' The next day the policeman was strolling in the same park when he saw the same man with the penguin. hiː went ʌp tuː hɪm ənd sed, 'dɪdnt aɪ tel juː tə teɪk ðat peŋgwɪn tuː ðə zuː?' 'Yes,' replied the man, 'ðats wɒt aɪ dɪd jestədeɪ ənd tədeɪ aɪm teɪkɪŋ hɪm tuː ðə sɪnəmə.'

4 Which is the odd word out, from the point of view of pronunciation? Use a dictionary which uses the IPA to help you. Write each word in the IPA.

a love, cove, dove   **c** bough, plough, through

b lose, rose, chose   **d** wonder, yonder, ponder

Vocabulary: Learning words in groups

Psychologists say that you can help yourself to learn new vocabulary more effectively by grouping words and expressions in some way that makes sense to you. You can make connections in many different ways – you may have met the words you are learning in the same text, for example, or they may be associated because of their meaning or because they have something grammatical or structural in common. Or they may simply have a personal association for you which might have no apparent logic for someone else.

1 Some students who studied the news broadcast in this unit decided to learn words in the following groups. Can you see what the association was for them between all the words and expressions in each group?

a earthquake, devastation, to creak, inevitable, insurance claims
b earthquake, aftershocks, tremor, epicentre, Richter scale, seismology
c earthquake, landslide, hurricane, flood, drought
d to quake, to shiver, to tremble, to shudder, to quiver
e earthquake, to earth a plug, to unearth, where/how/why on earth, down-to-earth, to cost the earth
f earthquake, landslide, thunderstorm, sunstroke, rainhat, waterfall
g devastation, inflation, multiplication, operation, adoration
h earthquake, steel, snore, dash, volcano

2 ▣ Now listen to the second news item again. Think about words you could learn which have the associations suggested below.

a Five words or expressions used in the news item.
b Five words or expressions connected with the economy.
c Five words or expressions based on the word *hope*.
d Five adjectives which can be used with the noun *rise*.
e Three synonyms for the verb *claim*.
f Three other nouns that can be followed by an infinitive like *a reason to believe*.

Reading: The news in Britain

1 Read this text which was written in the early 1990s about the lack of independence of the press in Britain. It is concerned with the nature of democracy and power in contemporary Britain. Then answer the questions which follow.

The owners (of newspapers) naturally want to use their papers to fortify their business empires. The Murdoch press, led by *The Times* and the *Sun*, dutifully boost their master's Sky Television and attack its main rival, the BBC. The *Telegraph* is encouraged by (its Canadian owner) Conrad Black to be 'correct' in its international alignment, supporting the United States government, the National Party in South Africa or Likud in Israel. Among daily papers only the *Independent* and the *Guardian* are independent of corporate pressures. In the age of information, media power becomes more valuable everywhere. Like railways in the last century, it can provide keys to other kingdoms: not just to politics or peerages, but to oil fields, television stations or the rest of the entertainments industry.

As the press boomed through the eighties, it became less distinct from other powers. While tabloids came closer to showbiz, most 'posh papers' came closer to politics and business: their journalists became less bohemian and more conformist – they wore dark suits, drank less and sat in front of computer screens. Prosperity has extracted a price. Most newspapers are much more conservative than their readers or journalists (half of the *Telegraph* journalists are anti-Tory). The bias and stridency of their election propaganda in 1992 amazed foreign observers. 'It is journalism of a kind now hardly known in the United States,' wrote Anthony Lewis in the *New York Times*, 'grotesquely partisan, shamelessly advancing one party's cause. And almost all of it is pro-Conservative.' When Neil Kinnock (the leader of the Labour Party during the 1992 election)

blamed the Tory press for his defeat, the *Sun* retorted that the complaint had 'not a word of truth', yet after the election it had boasted 'IT'S THE SUN WOT WON IT!' And Major (the Conservative Party leader) was quick to thank the editors of the *Sun*, *Daily Mail* and *Daily Express* – two of them Tory knights – for their support.

a What point is the text making about the owners of newspapers in Britain in the first paragraph?

b How do newspapers today resemble railways in the nineteenth century?

c What does the second paragraph tell us about the economic situation in the eighties in Britain? How did this affect journalists?

d What does the writer mean by the first sentence of the third paragraph?

e What point of difference is drawn between British and US journalism today?

f What inconsistency in the *Sun*'s position does the third paragraph illustrate? Which of their two contradictory statements do you think the writer believes more? What in the text indicates that he holds this opinion?

2 Underline any words or expressions in the text whose meaning you did not know before studying the text – and perhaps are still not sure about. Then do the following exercises.

1 Choose a word or expression which you feel is best explained by a translation into your own language. Write it down in that way.

2 Choose a word or expression which you feel could be usefully written down in an example sentence. Write it down in that way.

3 Choose a word or expression which you feel could be usefully written down with a definition of its meaning (in English). Write it down in that way.

4 Choose a word or expression which you feel can be explained by a drawing or diagram. Illustrate it in that way.

5 Choose a word which you feel needs to be written down in three or four different collocations. Write it down in that way.

6 Choose a word which you feel could be usefully written down with other words formed from the same root. Write down those words.

7 Choose a word or expression which you feel needs to be written down with a note on some aspect of its grammar. Write it down with the appropriate note.

8 Choose a word or expression which you feel needs to be written down with a note on its register. Write it down with the appropriate note.

9 Choose a word or expression which you feel needs to be written down with a note on its pronunciation. Write it down with the appropriate note.

10 Earlier in this unit you looked at ways of learning words in groups. Can you find a way of grouping all the words and expressions you have written down in different ways in this exercise?

Speaking: Bias in the news

Discuss the following questions.

a Is the situation described in the text about the press in Britain to any extent true of your own country or any other countries you know about?

b How can these factors influence what is printed in newspapers or broadcast in the news on radio or TV?
- big business
- government
- political or religious ideology
- desire to sell papers or increase ratings
- desire to improve or educate society
- striving after the truth
- advertisers

c How important do you think each of these factors is in your country and/or in any other country you know well?

d What criteria do you think news editors use when deciding whether to report a story in a newspaper or on radio or TV?

e Do you think those criteria are the best ones to base their decisions on?

f Have you ever been involved personally in a situation that was reported in the news? If so, how accurate were the reports?

g What are the arguments for and against any kind of censorship of the news?

Study skills: The news

1 Do you think these statements are true or false? Discuss with the other students in the class.

a Listening to or watching the news in English every day/week is a good idea because you may already have an idea of the content of the news items.

b Listening to or watching the news regularly is a good idea because the same vocabulary is regularly repeated.

c Listening to or watching the news regularly in English is difficult to do if you are not in an English-speaking country.

d Listening to or watching the news regularly in English is a good idea because broadcasts are so frequent you can get into the habit of listening at a regular time that is convenient for you, e.g. as you are getting up or at bed-time.

2 Discuss the following questions with other students.

a Do you like to keep up with the news in your own language?

b To what extent do you currently follow the news in English?

c Would it be useful for you personally to try to keep up with the news in English? If so, how could you most easily do so?

The main aspects of language worked on in this unit are:

- language reference books, especially English–English dictionaries
- stress in words and sentences
- prepositions
- collocations

Reading: Language reference books

1 There are a lot of different kinds of language reference books. Some useful ones are:

- a bilingual dictionary;
- a monolingual learner's dictionary;
- a picture or photo dictionary;
- a lexicon;
- a grammar reference book.

Answer these questions.

a Which of these do you have easy access to?

b How often do you use them?

c Do you have access to any other types of language reference materials?

d What sorts of things do you use language reference materials for?

2 Can you identify which language reference books (from the list in Exercise 1) the extracts on the right come from?

a **hap-py** [PLEASED] /'hæp·i/ *adj* **-ier, -iest** feeling, showing or causing pleasure or satisfaction • *You look happy!* • *It was a very happy marriage.* • *Stella didn't have a very happy childhood.* • *School days are said to be the happiest days of your life.* • *Nicki seems a lot happier since she met Steve.* • *You'll be happy* **to** *know that Jean is coming with us.* [+ to infinitive] • *I won't come with you to the cinema, but I'm perfectly happy* **to** (= I will willingly) *pick you up afterwards.* [+ to infinitive] • *I'm so happy* **(that)** *everything is working out for you.* [+ (that) clause] • *Barry seemed happy enough working 60 hours a week.* [+ v-ing] • *Are you happy* **about/with** (= satisfied with) *your new working arrangements?* • *Your mother's not going to be very happy when she sees the mess you've made!* • *(fml) The manager will be happy* (–able) **to** *see you this afternoon.* [+ to infinitive] • *(humorous)* A marriage is sometimes referred to as **the happy day**: *So when's the happy day then?* • *(humorous)* The birth of a child is sometimes referred to as **the happy event** (*Am also* **the blessed event**). • If someone is **happy-go-lucky**, they do not plan very much and they accept what happens without being made anxious by it: *You need to be a bit happy-go-lucky in this business.* • A **happy hour** is a period of time, usually in the early evening, when drinks are sold cheaply in a bar or a PUB. • *(approving)* A **happy medium** is a state or way of doing something which avoids being extreme, often combining the best of two opposite states or ways of doing something: *I try to* **strike a** (= achieve a) *happy medium when I'm on holiday, and spend half my time doing things and the other half just relaxing.*

b **rule** [I∅; T1] to have and use the highest form of social power over (a country, people, etc), esp as a king or queen: *Long ago kings ruled with complete power, but nowadays most countries are governed by parliaments, assemblies, or councils. He ruled the country well.*

govern [I∅; T1] to control the political affairs of (a country, etc and its people): *The Queen is said to rule Britain, but it is her prime minister who actually governs (the country).*

reign [Wv4;I∅ (over)] to be king or queen: *The Queen of Great Britain reigns but does not govern. The king reigned over his people for 15 years. Queen Elizabeth was the reigning monarch* [⇒ C96] *at that time.*

run [T1] *often infml* to be in control of and cause to work: *Who is running this country? The various ministers run their departments of state.*

preside over [v prep T1] *fml* to run or administer: *He presided over the affairs of the nation for 40 years.*

police [T1] to control very firmly, with or like a police force: *He policed those lawless places until men could feel safe again. Who will police the country if he takes his soldiers abroad?*

c Here is a list of nouns which usually or often have 'on' after them:

assault	comment	curb	hold	restriction
attack	concentration	dependence	insistence	stance
ban	constraint	effect	reflection	tax
claim	crackdown	embargo	reliance	

Here is a list of nouns which are usually followed by one of two prepositions. The list indicates the choice of prepositions available:

agreement about	battle against	debate about	transition from
agreement on	battle for	debate on	transition to
argument against	case against	decision about	
argument for	case for	decision on	

Here is a list of other nouns usually followed by a preposition.

complex about	safeguard against	excerpt from	awareness of
crime against	anger at	freedom from	authority over
grudge against	bond between	quotation from	control over
insurance against	departure from	foray into	
reaction against	escape from	relapse into	

3 **Which of the books, a to c, would you find useful if you wanted to know the following?**

- when to use articles with abstract nouns;
- whether to use *myself* with the verb *enjoy*;
- what the exact difference is between two rather similar words;
- which prepositions follow the words *to depend, independent* and *independence*;
- an alternative to the word *maintain*, which you've already used twice in a composition.

4 **Look again at the extracts. Answer these questions.**

a Look at the dictionary entry for *happy*. Which phrase in it do you like best?
b How could you use each of the *ruling and administering* verbs to describe the situation in a country you know well)?
c Can you identify any similarity of meaning between any of the words in the *on* box?

Reading: Encyclopedia of the English Language

A very interesting reference book about the English language is the *Cambridge Encyclopedia of the English Language*.

1 **Read the following extract. Then answer the questions which follow.**

AMERICA TALKING

The new American vocabulary of the 19th century came from a mixture of sources. Spanish and Native American words were especially influential, but also many older English words came to be used with new senses or in new phrases. The opening up of the West was one major factor in lexical expansion; the arrival of waves of immigrants, towards the end of the century, was another (p. 94).

bronco (1850), cattle town (1881), chaps (1870), corral (1829), cowpoke (1880), dogie (1888), dude (1883), lariat (1831), lasso (1819), maverick (1867), ranch (1808), range (1835), roundup (1876), rustler (1882), six shooter (1844), stampede (1843), tenderfoot (1849), trail boss (1890)

The Melting Pot

This phrase, the title of Israel Zangwill's 1909 successful play, itself became part of the new lexicon, and well summarizes the effect on American English of thousands of new words and phrases from German, Italian, Yiddish, and other European languages, as well as the jargon of the immigration process. Not everything was pleasant. In particular, there was a marked increase in the number of offensive racial labels.

delicatessen (1893), Hunk (1896), kike (1880s), kindergarten (1862), naturalization papers (1856), Polack (1879), spaghetti (1880s), spiel (1894), tutti-frutti (1876), wop (1890s).

(After S. B. Flexner, 1976.)

THE COW BOY COOK.

MYTH OR REALITY?

brave (1819), firewater (1817), Great Spirit (1790), Indian Agency (1822), medicine dance (1805), peace pipe (1860), reservation (1789), smoke signal (1873)

These words represent a fairly late stage of development in the lexicon of Native American affairs. Many native words entered the language during the period of first encounter: for example, *moccasin, papoose, powwow, wigwam,* and *tomahawk* are all 17th-century borrowings.

In the later period, many of the words put into the mouths of native people were invented or popularized by white authors who imagined that this was how 'Indians' ought to talk. Examples include *How!* (as a greeting), *heap big,* and *Great White Father. Happy Hunting Ground* is known from Washington Irving (1837); *paleface, war path,* and *war paint* are from James Fenimore Cooper (1820s). Myth or reality, they became part of the American lexicon nonetheless.

a Which languages provided some 'new' words for English in America?

b Which two historical events were important factors in the development of the language?

c What do the words listed under the first section of the text indicate about the lives of those who coined them?

d The phrase *the melting pot* is often used to describe the USA. What does it mean – literally and metaphorically?

e What point does the author make about the language which suggests that the country was a melting pot?

f What point does he make about the language which perhaps suggests that it was not totally successful as a melting pot?

g What is the *myth or reality* referred to in the sub-heading? What was real and what was myth?

h What do all the Native American words and expressions listed in this part of the text mean?

2 Good monolingual dictionaries are particularly precious for students. Ask your teacher to recommend a dictionary of this kind.

Use a monolingual dictionary to find the answers to the following questions.

a Where can you find the list of IPA symbols used by the dictionary?

b Look at the Contents page. What interesting information does the dictionary include apart from its alphabetic lists of words? (For example, what appendices does it have?)

c How do you pronounce the word *moustache*?

d Which preposition would be used in this sentence: *Old people can be very susceptible .... colds in winter.*

e What is the past simple form of the verb *to strive*?

f What do the letters *NATO* stand for?

g What animals do you find in (a) herds, (b) flocks and (c) shoals?

h What do we sometimes pay, apart from money or bills?

i What words can be formed from the root *compare*? Can you find at least one noun, two adjectives and one adverb? Remember to look at the entries both just before and just after *compare* itself.

j How many different meanings does the word *strike* have?

k What does the prefix *mis-* mean when it is added to a word?

l Give five different nouns (not including people) which go well with the adjective *rich*, e.g. *rich vocabulary*.

3 The following text about ghost words from the *Cambridge Encyclopedia of the English Language* has been printed below with three spelling mistakes, three mistakes with prepositions and three mistakes when the wrong word (from the right root) has been used. Use a dictionary to help you work out what the mistakes are.

A ghost word is one which has never existed in real life but which nevertheless turns out in a dictionary. It often happens because lexicographers are humane and make mistakes. An error in copying, typing, programming or fileing can easily lead for a false spelling or hyphenation and sometimes even a completly fictional item. Once the dictionary has appeared, however, its 'authority' will then make readers assume that the form is genuine. Some people may begin to use it. Certainly other lexicographers will notice it and it may then find its way into other dictionaries.

Such was the history of *Dord*; in the early 1930s the office preparing the second editor of *Webster's New International Dictionary* held a file of abreviations, one of which was 'D' or 'd' for density. When the work was published in 1934, the item appeared as *Dord* and gave the meaning *density*. Before long, the word was appearing on other dictionaries too.

Belgium's population dord is very high.

Speaking: Stress

1 Discuss the following questions with a partner.

a What does *stress* mean when we are talking about the pronunciation of a word with more than one syllable? Look it up in a dictionary if you are not sure.

b Where is the stress in the word *emphatic*?

c As we saw in the previous unit, dictionaries tell you how to pronounce a word. They also tell you which is the stressed syllable in a word of more than one syllable. Look at the dictionary extract at the beginning of this unit. How does it indicate stress?

d Do you use a different dictionary? If so, look at it. Does it indicate word stress in the same way?

2 ▭ Listen to these words. Mark where the stress falls, using the system used by your dictionary.

ɪntrəstɪŋ	teləfəʊn
resɪpi	təlefənɪst
kətæstrəfi	mæθəmætɪks
saɪkɒlədʒi	mæθəmətɪʃən
saɪkəlɒdʒɪkəl	ɪlɪməneɪt
fəʊtəgraːf	ɪlɪməneɪʃən
fətɒgrəfi	prəpəʊz
fəʊtəgræfɪk	prɒpəzɪʃən

3 Look up the word *record* (both as a noun and a verb) in your dictionary. What do you notice about its stress?

The following words have a similar stress pattern – with the stress on the first syllable when the word is a noun and on the second syllable when it is a verb.

conduct	conflict	contest	export
decrease	desert	import	increase
insult	permit	present	progress
protest	convert	reject	subject
suspect	transfer	transport	upset

4 Look at the 21 words in Exercise 3 (including *record*) and, to help learn them, group them in any way that seems logical to you.

5 ▭ Where do you think the stress will be on the underlined words in the sentences below? Check your answers by listening to the tape.

a The soldier <u>deserted</u> when he heard he was being posted to the <u>desert</u>.

b Crime has been <u>increasing</u> perhaps because there has been a <u>decrease</u> in job opportunities for school-leavers.

c On behalf of the judges, I should like to <u>present</u> the winner of the <u>contest</u> with a medal.

d The country's <u>imports</u> have to be <u>transported</u> a long way from the ports to the population centres.

e It is wrong that any British <u>subjects</u> should be <u>subjected</u> to such treatment in their own country.

f He felt he had been <u>insulted</u>, but his <u>protests</u> only led to further <u>conflict</u> between them.

6 Answer these questions.

a What does the word *stress* mean when we are talking about the pronunciation of a whole sentence or longer piece of connected speech?

b Which words in the sentence *Tom and Mary are sitting beside the pond in the garden* are most likely to be stressed?

c To some extent the words which are stressed in a sentence will depend on the context. What might be the context if particular stress is given to these words?

Mary
sitting
garden

7 ▭ Stress in sentences is not as fixed as stress in words. It can vary according to what the speaker wishes to convey. Listen to the sentence *Jamie drove Lucy to the cinema yesterday evening* spoken in seven different ways and decide what the implication of each way of speaking is. Write a to g beside the appropriate implication.

It was Jamie not Dick who drove her. ....
They didn't walk. ....
He didn't take Anna. ....
He didn't drive her back from the cinema. ....
They didn't go to the theatre. ....
It wasn't the day before yesterday. ....
It wasn't yesterday afternoon. ... .

8 ▭ Now practise reading the sentences stressing the appropriate words. Try doing it on your own first. Then listen to the tape and repeat what the speaker on the tape says.

a Patricia loves Marco. (It isn't Barbara who loves him.)
b Patricia loves Marco. (She doesn't just like him.)
c Patricia loves Marco. (She doesn't love John.)
d Sam is Canadian. (So is John.)
e Sam is Canadian. (Although you said he wasn't.)
f Sam is Canadian. (He isn't French.)
g The Browns went to live in London in 1994. (not the Smiths)
h The Browns went to live in London in 1994. (not just to visit it)
i The Browns went to live in London in 1994. (not in Edinburgh)
j The Browns went to live in London in 1994. (not in 1984)
k The Browns went to live in London in 1994. (not in 1993)

9 Choose one of the sentences in Exercise 7. Then say *Jamie drove Lucy to the cinema yesterday evening*, only thinking about the meaning of the sentence you chose, but not reading it. Can the other students recognise which sentence you chose and read it stressing the appropriate word or phrase?

Grammar: Prepositions

Using prepositions correctly is one of the most difficult aspects of using a foreign language and a good English–English dictionary, as we have seen, provides you with a lot of information about prepositions associated with particular words.

1 As we saw in the extract at the beginning of the unit, a good grammar book will also give you a lot of information about prepositions. Look again at that extract.

Agreement, *debate* and *decision* can be followed by *about* or *on*, but the difference in meaning is very small. However, there is a big difference when you use the different prepositions mentioned with the other words in the box.

Answer these questions.

a What is the difference between *an argument for revolution* and *an argument against revolution*?
b What is the difference between *the battle against democracy* and *the battle for democracy*?
c What is the difference between *the case for abortion* and *the case against abortion*?
d What does this suggest about the meaning of the word *against*?
e According to the extract, what other nouns are commonly associated with *against*? Does *against* have a similar meaning when used with these words?

2 Usually when a noun is followed by a particular preposition, any verb from the same root will – if it needs a preposition at all – take the same one; thus, *insistence on* and *to insist on*.

Answer these questions.

a Which of the words in the *agreement* box have an associated verb from the same root? Can it be used with both prepositions in the same way?

b Which of the verbs in the *complex* box have an associated verb from the same root? Which (if any) prepositions are these verbs used with?

3 A careless typist has missed out some of the prepositions in these sentences. Insert the correct prepositions where they are needed.

a There are a number of restrictions what you can import into most countries.

b She illustrated her essay with many apt quotations Shakespeare.

c Some people think that computers will be the solution their every problem.

d He still bears a grudge his brother for breaking his favourite train when they were children.

e His decision the matter will probably depend the advice which his wife offers him tonight.

f Some people argue that there is a strong case making soft drugs legal.

g Jane's dissertation concentrated the relationship between landlord and peasant in pre-emancipation Russia.

h John doesn't seem to have any control his children.

i People often say that there is a particularly strong bond grandparents and grandchildren.

j Richard has quite a complex being the only member of his family who did not go to university.

4 This letter appeared in the *Financial Times* recently. N.B. There were no prepositions or gaps in the original letter – the gaps have been added for the sake of the exercise.

Read the letter ignoring the gaps. How easy is it to understand? Use a dictionary to help you work out what prepositions are needed to write the letter in the standard way, i.e. with prepositions as required.

Sir,

It was .... surprise and pleasure that I took notice .... the headlines, 'Japan agrees stimulus deal' and 'NATO agrees air strike threat' (Feb. 10). Now I had regarded myself .... the only one who thought badly .... prepositions and proposed that they be done ....

These pesky words are a disgrace .... the language. They are susceptible .... misuse .... everyone and frequently get .... the way .... comprehension. We do not have to put .... this confusion. By dropping them .... our vocabularies, we see how easy it is to get .... our meaning and make do .... less space .... well; and I will argue vigorously .... anyone who disagrees .... me. Their elimination also allows one to dispense .... the annoying rule that one should never make use .... a preposition to end a sentence ....
Keep .... the good work!
Thomas Fuller
Paris, France

Vocabulary: Collocations

A very important function of dictionaries is that they can tell you which words are commonly used, or collocate, with which other words. Thus, if you look up *keep up*, for example, you may find *keep up the good work*, you may also find *to keep up a language, a house, an attack* and *keep old customs up.*

1 Look at the dictionary entry for *happy* at the beginning of the unit. Complete the sentences below.

a I know she is pregnant but when is the happy .... due?

b That pub has a happy .... from six o'clock; all the drinks are half price then.

c Jill wants to spend a month back-packing in the Himalayas while her husband would like to spend a week in a luxury hotel in France. They will have to try to find a happy ....

d He is very happy-go- .... in his attitude to life.

e Roy and Kate have just got engaged and they spend all their time discussing the arrangements for the happy ....

Roy and Kate have just got engaged …

2 Look at the lexicon extract on *ruling and administering* from the same page. Choose the best words to fit each of these sentences.

a Queen Elizabeth has .... since 1952, but no monarch has really .... Britain for centuries now.

b Who really .... the country? Is it government or is it big business?

c The political situation is very unstable there and government troops .... the streets every night.

d It is the prime minister and his or her cabinet which .... Britain rather than Parliament.

e The Russian tsar .... over his council of ministers and did not allow them much real power.

f Victoria was the .... monarch in Britain for most of the nineteenth century.

3 Word forks are ways of writing down sets of collocations (they look like forks with a prong for each collocation).

Use a dictionary to find collocations to complete the following word forks.

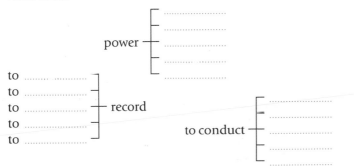

4 Look again at the text on American words from the *Cambridge Encyclopedia of the English Language*. Write out three collocations from the text, e.g. *melting pot*.

5 The strength of collocations becomes clear when we look at phrases which are not collocations. We do not say *thawing pot* or *mixing pot*, for instance, only *melting pot*. Note that phrases like *thawing pot* or *mixing pot* might be possible for a particular humorous or literary effect, but they are unlikely to be used in normal speech or writing; in normal speech and writing we tend to stick to standard collocations.

What words would you expect to replace the underlined words in these sentences? (The answers are all in work done in this unit.)

a You must reach a compromise; it is often necessary to try to find a <u>lucky</u> medium in life.

b Amazingly, the word *dord* managed to find its <u>path</u> into a number of dictionaries.

c In <u>actual</u> life we do not think about collocations; we just use them all the time.

d The prime minister <u>reigns over</u> the citizens of this country.

e She cut through the logs with a <u>knife</u>.

f Some supposedly Native American words were actually <u>made</u> by the writer Fenimore Cooper.

6 Now choose six words that you would particularly like to learn from this unit. Use a dictionary and make a note of some collocations using those words.

Teach your collocations to other students in the class.

The main aspects of language worked on in this unit are:

- listening to advertisements
- error correction
- adverbials expressing attitude
- positive and negative words
- keeping your eyes and ears open

Warm-up: Advertising

Discuss the following questions in groups.

a Have you ever been persuaded to buy anything or do anything because of an advertisement? If so, tell each other about some examples of how you were influenced.

b Are there any particular advertisements (from TV, radio or the press) which you can remember for some reason? Why exactly are they so memorable?

c Have you ever seen or heard of some unusual ways of advertising something? If so, what?

d What arguments can you think of in favour of advertising? What arguments can you think of against advertising?

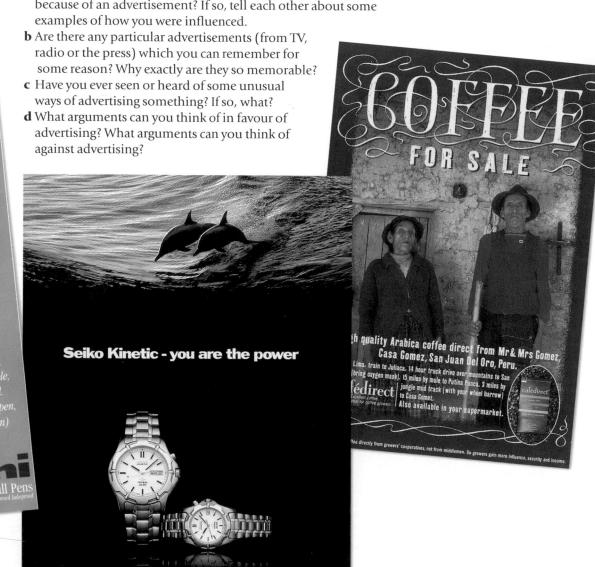

Seiko Kinetic - you are the power

Reliable, dependable, faithful. (We said pen, not men)

uni
Rollerball Pens
Waterproof leakproof fadeproof

http://www.uni-pen.co.uk

COFFEE FOR SALE

High quality Arabica coffee direct from Mr & Mrs Gomez, Casa Gomez, San Juan Del Oro, Peru.

Lima, train to Juliaca. 14 hour truck drive over mountains to San (bring oxygen mask). 15 miles by mule to Putina Punca. 3 miles by jungle mud track (with your wheel barrow) to Casa Gomez. Also available in your supermarket.

cafédirect
Excellent coffee. Ideal for coffee growers.

coffee directly from growers' cooperatives, not from middlemen. So growers gain more influence, security and income.

Listening: Radio adverts

1 ▣ Listen to five radio adverts and complete the table.

Type of product/ service offered	Name of company	Contact phone number or address

2 Answer the following questions.

a Which of the adverts on the tape did you find most persuasive and which least persuasive? Why?

b Here are some techniques which the creators of radio (and other) adverts often use to attract people's attention. Which of the techniques did the writers of these adverts for the radio use to make their adverts more appealing?
- alliteration
- catchy slogan
- dramatic incident
- exaggeration of product's qualities
- free offer
- humour
- jingle
- promise of a bargain
- repetition
- rhyme
- romantic interest
- scientific rationale for the effectiveness of the product
- snob appeal (i.e. appeal to people's desire to be in society's elite)
- sound effects

c Can you think of any other devices that could be used to make a radio advert effective?

Vocabulary: Positive and negative words

Advertisers often use positive words to make what they are trying to sell sound more attractive.

Quite often in English, there are several words which convey a similar concept. For example, someone who is not fat can be described as *thin*, *skinny* or *slim*. *Thin* is a fairly neutral word but, if you call a thin person *slim*, you like their appearance; if you call them *skinny*, you do not. Advertisers of dieting products will, of course, prefer to use the more positive word *slim*.

1 What positive words were used in the *Ben's Cookies* advert to help promote the biscuits being sold?

2 Here are some sentences used by property or car sales staff in order to try to sell their accommodation or their cars. What do you think they might really mean?

Example: The rooms are very cosy.
The rooms are rather small.

a The kitchen has great character.
b The house is very conveniently located for the well-served station.
c The property is set in an attractively rural situation.
d The flat has enormous potential.
e The car is fitted with all the latest luxuries.
f This model is particularly compact.
g This car is a remarkable bargain.
h The car has a most unusual and stylish modern design.

3 Put the words in the box into pairs with similar meanings. In each case, decide whether the basic association is positive or negative. Mark any of the words which are particularly colloquial in register.

> ambitious   arrogant
> assertive   bossy
> broad-minded   brusque
> determined   extravagant
> frank   generous   obese
> odd   original
> pig-headed   plump
> pushy   self-assured
> thrifty   tight-fisted
> unprincipled

4 Job candidates have to give the names of referees who will write testimonials about their personal qualities. Traditionally, referees focus on the positive sides of someone's character. If they wish to say something that is not altogether positive, then they usually couch it in the most positive terms possible. Would the following sentences be appropriate for a formal letter of reference? If not, how could they be improved?

a John's odd ideas will be of value to any company where he works.
b Louise is always brusque, which is a great advantage for a personal assistant.
c William's pig-headed approach will ensure his success in any career.
d Sarah's arrogant manner makes her an ideal candidate for the post of unit manager.
e Ralph is very pushy and he will probably make it to the top of his chosen career.
f Harriet has always been bossy and so I have no hesitation in recommending her for the post of Sales Director.
g Jack's unprincipled approach has helped to make him a successful journalist.
h Sharon is very tight-fisted, an undeniable asset for a housekeeper.

Grammar: Adverbials expressing attitude

Some adverbs and adverbial expressions are used to express the speaker's attitude to what he or she is saying. For example:
Luckily, I went straight to Specter and Grant after my accident.
Task Force, *unfortunately*, is unable to suggest employment for you at the moment.

1 What do the adverbs *luckily* and *unfortunately* tell you about how the speaker feels about what is being said?

2 Look at this list of some of the most common adverbials used to express the speaker's attitude.

alas	anyway	astonishingly S	at least
coincidentally	conveniently	curiously	fortunately
frankly	honestly	in all honesty	in fairness
in my opinion O	in retrospect	incredibly	ironically
luckily P	mercifully	miraculously	mysteriously
naturally E	oddly	of course	on reflection
predictably	remarkably	sadly N	significantly
strangely	surprisingly	to my mind	typically
unbelievably	understandably	unexpectedly	unfortunately

Divide these adverbials into groups as indicated. In each case one has already been labelled for you. Do not put any letter beside any of the adverbials which you feel do not fit into any of these groups.

1 Mark with an S all the adverbials in the list above which indicate that the speaker is surprised or puzzled by what he or she is saying.
2 Mark with an E (for *expected*) all the adverbials that suggest that the speaker is not surprised by what he or she is saying.
3 Mark with an N all the adverbials that indicate that the speaker has negative (or sad) feelings about what he or she is saying.
4 Mark with a P all the adverbials which indicate that the speaker is pleased or relieved about what he or she is saying.
5 Mark with an O all the adverbials which emphasise that the speaker is giving his or her opinion when he or she speaks.

3 You probably did not mark all the adverbials used in the sentences below. They all have quite specific implications. Choose the implication or situation on the right which seems to match each of the sentences on the left.

a At least, he loves dogs.

b Anyway, he loves dogs.

c Conveniently, he loves dogs.

d Ironically, he loves dogs.

e In fairness, he loves dogs.

f Significantly, he loves dogs.

i This is a very important fact about him.

ii He's just been attacked by one.

iii He's marrying someone who has six.

iv I'm trying to see it from his point of view.

v I've just thought of this point to add.

vi He has this positive characteristic among his many failings.

4 Write each of the sentences below twice, adding two different attitude adverbials. What meaning do the adverbials give in each case?

a Task Force has found jobs for many local school-leavers.

b I was very sick after eating half a kilo of cookies one evening.

c It is not cheap to consult a good insurance company.

d The last second-hand car I bought lasted me ten years.

e The Kingsway Golf Centre is very good value.

…, he loves dogs!

Writing: Error correction

It is important to get into the habit of checking your own work. But it can often be easier to see mistakes which other people have made. Here are some examples of radio adverts for some evening classes being run at a local college. The adverts were prepared by students of English. In each advert there are several errors.

Underline the errors. What kind of error is each one – spelling, grammar or vocabulary?

Write the adverts out correctly.

a If you do not want to start loosing your knowledges of English or any other foreing language, enrol at an evening class this autumn.

b Don't be narrow-brained! Learn about the cultures of other countries at the Technical Colledge's new evening class on *Other Countries: There Customs and Cultures*. Give yourself a good basement for a more advanced course studying World Societies, which we plan inaugurating next year.

c What do you must do if you want to enrol on one of our course? Festival, you should come along on our registration day for giving your name to one of our staff. Curiously, it's easy. When you will arrive at the entrance to the college, just follow the signs saying 'Evening Classes'.

d I made a course in economical history last year and, in my mind, it was an excruciating course. I would recommend it to anyone with an interest for history.

e Perhaps you did not study for a long time. Never mind. You will soon get used to attend classes and write essays again. And we are sure that you will find any class what you choose mysteriously enjoiable.

f Do you need to become more arrogant? Are you worried that you are getting obese? Do you wish you are more pushier? We have evening classes for you – in Assertiveness for Weight-watchers and in Acheiving your Ambitions. And in many more subjects too. Just come along and make your pick.

Speaking: Making a radio advert

Work in groups to make a
radio advert by following
these instructions.

1 Work with three or four other students. Choose a product or service – for example, a local place of entertainment, your school or college or something offered for sale by a company that you have personal connections with.
2 Try to use some of the advertising devices and some of the vocabulary items discussed in this unit and design an advert for your product or service.
3 When you have prepared your script, check it as critically as you can. Correct and improve it where necessary.
4 If possible record your advert.
5 Play it to other students in your class and ask them to comment on both its qualities as an advert and the extent to which it gives an accurate picture of the product or service.

Study skills: Keeping your ears and eyes open

You can learn a lot of English by being aware of the English you come across – and you can do this even when you are not in an English-speaking environment.

Make a note of any new words and expressions you meet, any language points that puzzle you or any other interesting uses of the language that you encounter.

1 Fill in the questionnaire below.

Is English ever to be heard or seen in the following situations in your country? Tick all the boxes which apply.

	YES	NO
Are films in English ever shown on your country's TV or in the cinema?	☐	☐
Do you hear pop songs in English?	☐	☐
Is it possible to tune in to English-language TV?	☐	☐
Can you borrow English-language books and/or video films from a library?	☐	☐
Is it possible to buy English-language newspapers or magazines?	☐	☐
Is English ever used by the media in your country?	☐	☐
English has taken an enormous number of words and expressions from a wide range of other languages. Does your language ever use any English words and expressions?	☐	☐
Do you – or could you – ever come into contact with English-speaking people visiting or working in your country?	☐	☐
Do you ever overhear English on the street or in any other public place?	☐	☐
Do you ever see English used in advertisements or notices?	☐	☐

2 Compare your answers to the questionnaire above with a partner. In each case where you have ticked a *yes* box, discuss these questions.

a How frequently and how easily can you see or hear this kind of English?
b What could you learn from this use of English?
c What could you do to help yourselves make the most of this kind of situation?

The main aspects of language worked on in this unit are:
- sayings
- writing a story
- using sayings in conversation
- gerunds

Warm-up: Sayings

1 Answer these questions with a partner.

  a What is a saying?
  b Can you translate one or two famous sayings or quotations from your own language into English?
  c Do you know any English sayings or quotations?

2 Later on in this unit you will do some work on sayings from your own language. At home, find two or three more sayings from your own language that particularly appeal to you. Translate them into English. Bring them to class. You will use them in Speaking Exercise 2 on page 33.

Reading: Well-known English sayings

A quotation or saying, in the sense used in this unit, is a memorable, well-expressed phrase or sentence which is taken up and repeated by others because it conveys an idea in a particularly effective way. Some quotations are so famous that they are probably familiar to every native speaker. For example, what British person does not know Shakespeare's famous line where Hamlet considers suicide: *To be or not to be, that is the question*?

1 Read the sayings, a–l, below and match them to the interpretations, 1–12.

  a 'Parents are the last people on earth who ought to have children.' (Samuel Butler)
  b 'No man thoroughly understands a truth until he has contended against it.' (Ralph Waldo Emerson)
  c 'Zoo: an excellent place to study the habits of human beings.' (Evan Esar)
  d 'She got her good looks from her father – he's a plastic surgeon.' (Groucho Marx)
  e 'Those who can do, those who can't teach.' (George Bernard Shaw)
  f 'Never put off till tomorrow what you can do the day after tomorrow.' (Mark Twain)
  g 'I'm living so far beyond my income that we may almost be said to be living apart.' (Saki)
  h Swans sing before they die.
    'Twere no bad thing
    Should certain persons die
    Before they sing. (S. T. Coleridge)
  i 'Do what you can with what you have where you are.' (Theodore Roosevelt)
  j 'Work is the refuge of people who have nothing better to do.' (Oscar Wilde)
  k 'Is it progress if a cannibal uses a knife and fork?' (Stanislaw J. Lec)
  l 'Workers of the world, unite; you have nothing to lose but your chains. You have the world to gain.' (Karl Marx)

  1 By joining together, oppressed people can become free.
  2 I'm spending far more money than I actually possess.
  3 Make the best of your own personal circumstances.
  4 No one is much good at bringing up their own children.
  5 Only people who don't know how to spend their time in an enjoyable way do any work.
  6 People are just like animals in their behaviour.
  7 Procrastinate as much as you can.
  8 She has had a lot of cosmetic surgery.
  9 Some people sing atrociously badly.
  10 Teachers are themselves not much good at doing what they teach others to do.
  11 Teaching primitive people sophisticated manners may not be real progress.
  12 You need to argue against something to understand it fully.

2 Discuss these questions with a partner.

  a Do you think the interpretations always accurately convey what the original saying intended? If not, why not?
  b Why are the sayings quoted more effective than their interpretations?

Vocabulary: From the sayings

1 Find words or expressions in the sayings in Reading Exercise 1 which match the following definitions (in the context of the sayings):

  a to assert that something is true
  b the last resort
  c person who eats human flesh
  d appearance
  e postpone
  f it would be
  g more than what is received
  h what restricts a person

2 Sayings often help to make their point by using particularly apt vocabulary. Here are some quotations about work. In each case, one of the words which help to give the saying its point has been removed. These words are in the box above the quotations. Can you put them back in the right places?

> believer   sin   capable   eventually
> expands   faithfully   intoxicate
> particularly   really   supposed

a Work .... so as to fill the time available for its completion.

b Work with some men is as besetting a .... as idleness.

c They .... themselves with work so they won't have to see how they really are.

d By working .... eight hours a day, you may .... get to be a boss and work twelve hours a day.

e I'm a great .... in luck and I find the harder I work the more I have of it.

f Most people like hard work; .... when they are paying for it.

g Anybody is .... of doing any amount of work provided it isn't the work he is .... to be doing.

h Nothing is .... work unless you would rather be doing something else.

3 Check your understanding of the sayings about work by answering the following questions about them.

a Which of these sayings essentially have a positive attitude towards work and which of them are more negative or cynical?

b Have you any personal experience of the truth of any of them? If so, which and what experience have you had or heard of that makes you feel there is truth in this saying?

Speaking: Sayings in conversation

1 How quickly can you bring a saying into your conversation? Your teacher will give you instructions for this exercise.

2 Work in groups. Tell each other about some of the sayings you have brought in (and/or the sayings you used in Exercise 1) and discuss these questions.

a Why do you think they are particularly effective?

b Is there anything that you particularly like about them?

c Can you imagine yourself ever being able to bring any of these sayings into a conversation? If so, when might this be possible?

d Choose your group's top two sayings to present to the rest of the class.

Grammar: Gerunds or *-ing* nouns

If you want to make a particular verb do the work of a noun, i.e. be the subject or object of another verb or follow a preposition, then you use the *-ing* form or gerund of the verb.

1 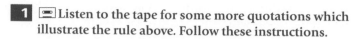 Listen to the tape for some more quotations which illustrate the rule above. Follow these instructions.

1 Write down the sayings which you hear.
2 Underline the gerund in each of the examples.
3 Explain the meaning of the saying in your own words.

2 Which gerunds do you think originally completed these sayings?

a .... people is wrong.
b A university should be a place of light, of liberty and of ....
c The greatest part of a writer's time is spent in ....
d To talk without .... is to shoot without ....
e .... is the ruin of all happiness.
f .... is such sweet sorrow.
g It is preoccupation with property, more than anything else, that prevents men from .... freely and nobly.
h The saddest thing I can imagine is to get used to .... luxuries.

3 Some gerunds can also be used as countable nouns, e.g. *I've arranged a meeting with the sales department tomorrow.* Sometimes the meaning (and the word *meaning* itself is another example of this type of noun) is more specific than the meaning of the original verb.

What do the following underlined countable gerunds in these sentences mean?

a We have a <u>saying</u> just like that in my language too.
b There's going to be a second <u>showing</u> of the film tomorrow evening.
c I'll get the job. I've got a <u>feeling</u> in my bones about it.
d The second <u>sitting</u> for dinner will start in five minutes' time.
e A gale <u>warning</u> was issued at ten o'clock GMT.
f The <u>hearing</u> is scheduled to begin next Monday.
g Take the first <u>turning</u> on the left.
h Do you like my <u>drawing</u>?
i The hotel stands in a spectacular <u>setting</u> on the edge of the lake against a backdrop of mountains.

4 Any preposition is followed by either a noun or a verbal noun, i.e. a gerund. Complete the following sentences with any appropriate expression using a gerund.

a Jack won the race in spite of …
b You can use a Swiss Army Knife for …
c You can't make an omelette without …
d John is not good at many practical things around the house like …
e Jo wasn't a very good swimmer because of …
f I decided to spend the evening at home instead of …
g Susie has many talents besides …
h Fiona succeeded in becoming managing director of her own company without …

Jack won the race in spite of …

5 Many verbs are associated with particular prepositions. For example, the police might *suspect* a criminal *of committing* a crime and, if they are convinced that he is guilty they will *charge* him *with committing* that crime.

Add both a preposition and an appropriate gerund phrase to complete each of these sentences. Don't use an ordinary noun after your preposition even though that would, of course, be possible too.

a I don't believe …
b My family are thinking …
c Bill was prevented …
d Sarah was accused …
e Jane was complimented …
f Her interest in China stems …
g These vitamin tablets are supposed to protect you …
h The teacher always insists …
i I really object …
j We must congratulate Charlie …
k The music distracted me …
l I am looking forward …

Writing: A proverb story

1 Proverbs are sayings that are so well-known that, when we use them in conversation, we often use just the first few words of the proverb and our listeners will understand the rest. The words on the left are those that are often all we say and the words on the right are those that the listener understands. Match the opening words with the correct ending.

It's the last straw
A bird in the hand
When the cat's away
There's many a slip
Don't cross your bridges
You can lead a horse to water
Too many cooks
Many hands
Don't count your chickens
People who live in glass houses

the mice will play.
before they're hatched.
that breaks the camel's back.
before you come to them.
make light work.
spoil the broth.
is worth two in the bush.
shouldn't throw stones.
but you can't make it drink.
'twixt cup and lip.

2 Answer these questions.

a What is the literal meaning of each of the above proverbs?
b Can you imagine a situation where each of them might be used?
c Is there a similar proverb in your language?

3 With a partner write a story which leads up to one of these proverbs as its last line. If possible use some of the gerund constructions we have worked on in this unit.

Read your story to other students in the class but stop before the proverb at the end. Can the other students guess the proverb which is the climax of your story?

When the cat's away …

The main aspects of language worked on in this unit are:
- listening to songs
- rhyme
- non-standard grammar
- affixes
- learning from songs

Warm-up: Songs

Discuss with two or three other students:
What kind of songs (if any) do you like to listen to:

- at a party?
- on a journey?
- when you get home in the evening?
- first thing in the morning?
- when you're studying?
- at a concert?

Listening: Songs

1 ▭ You are going to listen to a song. You have some of the words written below but most of the lines are incomplete. Listen to the song as often as you need to in order to complete the lines.

Coope, Boyes & Simpson

Skeeter Davis

Growing up in hard times
Means you're often
But though
You remember

You gotta make it
Make it

Now when
They would temper
If something
For they took

Now the watchword
And if something
But when
Well, you'll see

Now politicians tell you
They can see
But if greed's
How can things

2 ▭ Here is another song, *The End of the World*, a country music song sung by Skeeter Davis. Listen and then answer the questions.

a How is the singer feeling?
b Why is the singer feeling this way?
c What questions does the singer ask?

3 How much can you remember of the words of the song? With a partner, write down what you can recall.

▭ Listen again and complete the words.

4 Discuss with a partner.

a Do the two songs have anything in common?
b Do you like these songs? Why, or why not?

Speaking: Rhyme

When you were trying to work out what the words were in the songs above, you probably used rhyme to help you.

1 Give an example of rhyme from each of the two songs.

2 Here, written in the IPA, are some examples of words which are frequently found in songs. Say the words, then write them in their ordinary spelling. With a partner, find at least five rhymes for each of them.

a lʌv   **d** taɪm
b hɑːt   **e** juː
c dɪə   **f** miː

3 Play a rhyming game.

1 Sit in a circle. Your teacher will start by giving a word, e.g. *could*. The next person has to give a word that rhymes with could, e.g. *wood*.
2 Go round the circle with each person adding a rhyme until someone cannot think of another rhyme. That person is out.
3 The person who is out provides a word to start the next round of the game, which continues until only one person is left.
4 No word may be used in the same game more than once.
5 You may challenge a person who uses a word which you think does not exist – if they don't know the meaning of that word, they are out.
6 Anyone who pronounces a word incorrectly to make it appear to be a rhyme is out.

4 With a partner, write a short verse to go inside a card (a Valentine perhaps or some other kind of card for someone to send to a person they love). Use some of the rhymes you found in Exercise 2. Read your verse aloud to the class.

Grammar: Non-standard English

1 Songs sometimes use language that is not normally considered standard English. The exercise below gives some lines from songs which use typically non-standard English, for example, double negatives, loose pronunciation, the incorrect use of *like* as a conjunction rather than a preposition, the use of *ain't* to mean *am/is/are not*.

Write the lines in the standard way.

What typical non-standard characteristics do each of the lines exemplify?

a I wanna have your love.
b I'm gonna see that man of mine tonight.
c I ain't gonna love you no more.
d I feel like I'm asleep.
e Don't ya love me no more?
f Love me gentle, love me soft.
g I got a heart full of you.
h You and me gonna reach the stars.
i They never learn you love at school.

2 ⊟ Listen to the speaker on the tape and answer these questions.

a What examples of non-standard English do you hear?
b What should the speaker really have said in each case?

3 Read this text about two different ways of writing language from the *Cambridge Encyclopedia of the English Language* and answer these questions.

a What is the difference between a prescriptive and a descriptive grammarian?
b How would prescriptive and descriptive grammarians react to the language in Exercises 1 and 2?
c Can you think of any examples of usage in your own language which a prescriptive grammarian might condemn?

Prescriptivism is the view that one variety of language has an inherently higher value than others, and that this ought to be imposed on the whole of the speech community. It is an authoritarian view propounded especially in relation to grammar. The favoured variety is usually a version of the standard written language, especially as encountered in literature, or in the formal spoken language which most closely reflects literary style and it is presented in dictionaries, grammars and other official manuals. Those who speak and write in this variety are said to be using language 'correctly'; those who do not are said to be using it 'incorrectly'.

The alternative to a prescriptive approach is the descriptive approach associated mainly with modern linguistics. As the name suggests, its main aim is to describe and explain the patterns of usage which are found in all varieties of the language, whether they are socially prestigious or not. The approach recognises the fact that language is always changing and that there will accordingly always be variations in usage. Linguists do not deny the importance of the standard language, but they do not condemn as 'ugly', 'incorrect' or 'illogical' other dialects which do not share the same rules.

4 Native speakers are often taught about the grammar of English at school in a very prescriptive way and the sentences here illustrate the things which teachers are most likely to rail against. In each case, identify what the example of non-standard use is and change the sentence into the kind of English that teachers prefer.

a I hope to quickly finish writing my essay.
b Jack has approached the essay topic differently to the way I took it.
c None of us were there on time.
d We haven't done nothing wrong.
e The teacher took the books from Jack and I and promised to return them soon.
f That's the teacher who I gave my work to.
g Me and Sue finished work early today.
h Less people than were expected turned up at the meeting.

Vocabulary: Affixes

1 Affixes are either suffixes or prefixes. Work with a partner and answer these questions.

a What is a prefix? Find three examples of prefixes from the text on non-standard English.
b What is a suffix? Find three examples of suffixes from the text on non-standard English.

2 Knowing about affixes can often help you to work out what words mean. Answer these questions.

a What are the meanings of the prefixes and suffixes you found as examples in the previous exercise?
b Write down three more words as examples of each of the prefixes and suffixes you found.

3 Answer the following questions.

a What are the prefixes used in the words in the table?
b What meaning do they add to the root of the word?
c Write two examples of words using the same prefix with the same meaning.

Word	Prefix	Prefix meaning	Examples
post-graduate			
an ex-husband			
a submarine			
pseudo-scientific			
a bicycle			
a tricycle			
a unicycle			
monotonous			
to mistranslate			
to underpay			
to overeat			
pro-government			
anti-war			
to rewrite			
multi-media			
to disqualify			
incorrect			
uncomfortable			

4 Add a prefix to the incomplete words in order to complete the sentences.

a Left-wing parties tend to be ....-republican and ....-monarchy.

b Sue hasn't once seen her ....-boyfriend since they split up three months ago.

c They split up because of a silly ....understanding.

d You'd better ....connect the fridge before you try to repair it.

e He is so ....decisive; he takes ages even to choose what flavour of ice cream he wants.

f A ....lateral agreement is one involving a lot of different parties, whereas a ....lateral agreement involves only two parties.

g You shouldn't ....estimate John's talents. I think he'll surprise us all one of these days.

h The children are ....tired; that's why they are behaving so badly.

5 Answer these questions.

a What are the suffixes used in the words in the table?

b What meaning do they add to the root of the word?

c Write down two more examples of words using the same suffix with the same meaning.

Word	Suffix	Suffix meaning	Examples
a classmate			
a booklet			
a waitress			
bluish			
communism			
pardonable			
to popularise			
useful			
hopeless			
an employee			

6 Which of the above suffixes could be added to these roots in order to form a new word? In each case at least two words are possible. Explain the meanings of each of the words you form.

a work
b green
c escape
d flat
e author
f grace
g comfort
h social

7 Follow these instructions.

1 Choose ten words that you would particularly like to learn from the examples in the prefix and suffix boxes.

2 See if you can write two or three sentences including all these words.

3 Read your sentences to the other students in the class. Can they think of any of the other example words that could be included in your sentences?

Study skills: Learning from songs

1 Work in groups and answer these questions.

a Do you think that listening to songs can help you learn English? List as many different reasons why (or why not) as you can.
b What singers or songs would you recommend to someone who wants to improve their English through songs? Again list as many ideas as you can.
c Compare both your lists with those of other groups of students in the class and see how many different ideas the class got as a whole.

2 Follow these instructions.

1 If possible, bring a tape of a song with English words into class.
2 Play it to the class. To what extent can the words be easily understood? You might like to ask the rest of the class to help you to work out any words that you find difficult to distinguish.
3 If the words are all easy to follow, then ask the other students some questions about the content of your song – what it is about, what the mood is and so on.
4 When all the songs have been played, discuss which you liked best and why.

Deluged with information
The new mass media

The main aspects of language worked on in this unit are:	• reading and understanding the new mass media • planning and writing a discursive essay • the grammar of the infinitive • words from the same root

Warm-up: The information revolution

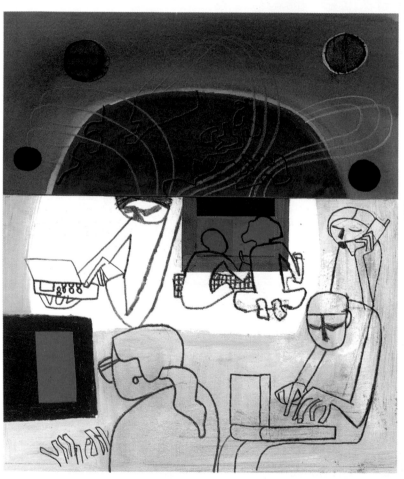

1 Discuss with a partner.

a It has been said that we are going through an 'information revolution' at the moment. What is meant by this term? What is revolutionary about the situation?

b Have you – or has anyone you know – had any personal experience of the 'information revolution'?

c How do you think the 'information revolution' might affect life in the future?

2 Answer these questions.

a What do you understand by the term *junk mail*? Why is it called *junk mail*? Why is it sent?

b Describe some examples of junk mail you have received.

c Junk mail takes advantage of modern technology too – it is infiltrating faxes and the Internet. Do you know of any examples of this?

Reading: A mail order catalogue

1 Advertisers are particularly keen exploiters of the information revolution. Look at the extracts from a mail order catalogue and answer these questions.

a Would you be tempted to order any of these products for yourself or any of your friends or family?

b Who do you think might buy each of these objects?

◄ *electronic* PEDOMETER

Measuring your performance is good motivation, as well as helping to make sure you don't overstretch yourself. This electronic pedometer can measure the miles and times, calculate the calories you're burning and count steps and distances in miles or kilometres. It also acts as a pacer, a stop watch and a countdown timer. Yet it is extremely light and clips easily to your clothing, handlebars and is even water resistant. Requires 2 x button batteries (supplied).

£15.95

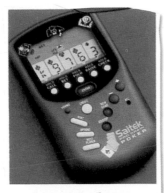

▲ *pro draw* POKER

Poker is the game of skill and nerve and now with this hand held game you can play it wherever you are. You have three real-life characters–the statistician, the daring player and the conservative one, to pit your wits against and play those essential mind games. This game captures the drama and tension of the real game while providing hints on strategy. Measures 15 x 7.5cm. Requires 1 x button battery (supplied).

£29.99

electronic tape MEASURE ►

This electronic measures utilises sound waves, so all you have to do is point it. The sound wave will bounce off the nearest object and the display will tell you the distance to the nearest inch or cm. Designed to measure any distance between 2 ft to 45 ft, horizontal, vertical or at any angle. It makes taking measurements so easy. Measures in feet or metres. Requires 1 x button battery.

£39.95

plant soil WATER REMINDER ►

Your plants can't tell you when they need watering but this handy device can. It will play a tune and flash to tell you it's time to give your plants some care and attention. Comes in a pack of three. Requires 2 x button batteries (supplied).

Pack of three

£12.95

£5.95

REALLY USEFUL SHOW

toolbox ▲ KEY RING

Closed this is a handsome and distinctive key ring but open it up and you have a sturdy screwdriver set with a choice of 4 screwdriver heads. Simply select the head you need and place it in the central position and you are ready for anything.

hat RADIO ►

When you're out and about but you still want to stay in tune with your favourite radio station, here's the stylish solution. This fashionable hat comes complete with its own built-in FM/AM radio. The antenna and radio tuning and volume controls are easily accessible, while the ear pieces drop down either side. The fashionable navy blue hat has an adjustable headband to suit all sizes. Requires 2 x AAA batteries (not supplied).

£16.95

REALLY USEFUL SHOW

£14.95

ALARM CLOCK *scent freshener* ▲

This clever little clock is a fully functioning alarm clock with a built-in motorised air freshener. Simply pour a little perfume into the pad in the dispenser and when the fan is switched on the air will be filled with your own choice of delightful scent.

2 Find words or expressions in the extracts from the catalogue to match each of these definitions (three from each advertisement).

do too much

fixes

not harmed by

risk-taking

compete mentally

suggestions

uses

make face in the desired direction

going straight up from the ground

good-looking

strong

well-prepared

convenient and useful

gadget

show lights

easily reached

can be modified to fit different sizes

not provided when you purchase the object

perfume

working in the normal way

small cushion

Listening: Surfing cyberspace

1 Answer these questions.

a What do you understand by the expression *surfing cyberspace*?

b Have you any personal experience of it? If so, what have you found in cyberspace and what have you enjoyed / not enjoyed about your experience of the Internet?

2 Follow these instructions.

1 🖳 Listen to two people discussing the Internet. Make a note of all the different uses of it which they mention.

2 Which of the uses they mention would you like to try and which do not interest you at all?

3 Which of the uses mentioned seem to you to be useful? Do any of them seem to be the electronic equivalent of 'junk mail'?

3 A lot of users of the Internet have very specific and unusual interests. Jane gave an example of pages about the character from children's stories, Winnie the Pooh. Imagine three possible uses of the Internet which would seem to you to be particularly weird. (Whatever you can imagine probably already exists!) Compare your ideas with those of other students in the class.

Grammar: The infinitive

1 The infinitive in English is the base form of the verb, used with *to* before it. Write down the sentences which use an infinitive in the extracts from the catalogue.

2 The infinitive can be used in English in the following ways. Which of these match the ways the infinitive is used in the sentences you wrote down?

1 As the subject of a clause (a role more usually carried out by the gerund).
2 Reporting an order or request.
3 After an ordinal number.
4 Indicating one's purpose.
5 Defining an impersonal structure.
6 Defining a rather general noun (e.g. *a chance to travel, a longing to return home, a desire to succeed*).
7 Defining an indefinite adverb or pronoun (*somewhere, nothing, anybody*, etc.).
8 Expanding on an adjective (e.g. *happy to meet you, sorry to have missed him*).
9 After one of a number of verbs (e.g. *ask, tell, order, remind*) with a direct object.
10 Explaining a compliment or criticism made about a person or thing.
11 In a passive sentence with one of a number of reporting verbs (e.g. *to be alleged, to be supposed*).
12 After one of a number of common verbs (e.g. *hope, manage, decide*) usually followed by the infinitive.
13 After a number of verbs used to express one's opinion about something or someone (e.g. *consider, believe*). The structure with the infinitive is more formal than the clause with *that* which is also possible with such verbs.

3 Here are some more examples of how the infinitive can be used in English. Match each of these to one of the types of usage listed in Exercise 2.

a I told you to stay here.
b There's no reason to believe he is lying.
c We're pleased to be of service.
d I've come to mend the cooker.
e We must find somewhere to live.
f I want to be told the truth.
g She is the ideal person to do the job!
h To err is human; to forgive divine.

i Yuri Gagarin was the first man to go into space.
j I always considered James to be an honest man.
k He is alleged to have stolen the car.
l We advise you not to leave your rooms.
m It's a good idea to write down new vocabulary that you especially want to learn.

4 Some nouns are frequently followed by a *to* infinitive (usage 6 from the list in Exercise 2). You had one example in sentence b above. The most common nouns often followed by an infinitive are:

> ability   attempt   chance   compulsion
> desire   disinclination   failure
> inability   need   opportunity   reason
> refusal   way   willingness
> unwillingness

Choose the most appropriate nouns from the box to complete each of the sentences.

a There must be a .... to solve the problem if we all put our minds to it.
b You should take every .... to travel when you are young.
c The company's .... to win the contract it was hoping for may well mean a fall in share prices.
d Pregnant women are said to have a .... to eat coal and other strange things.
e The mountaineer's .... to reach the top of Mount Everest without oxygen has failed.

5 Choose any appropriate infinitive phrase to complete the sentences.

a Julie has a remarkable ability ....
b I am very disappointed by your unwillingness ....
c Alice was very upset by her husband's refusal ....
d There is no need for you ....
e I would welcome the opportunity ....
f Mary is motivated by a strong desire ....

6 Which of the following verbs could – from a structural point of view – replace *considered* in the sentence below?

> reckoned
> thought
> presumed
>
> I always considered Pat to be an honest person.
>
> believed
> found
> judged
> held

How does the meaning change when different verbs are substituted for *considered*?

7 Work in teams of three or four students. Which team can most quickly think of each of the following?

a three adjectives to complete the sentence: I was very
.... to hear your news.

b three infinitive of purpose phrases to complete the sentence:
They went to the USA ....

c three verbs which could complete the sentence: I ....
him to be quiet.

d three infinitives to complete the sentence: She was the first
person ....

e three past participles which could complete the sentence: Smith
is .... to have gone to Ireland.

f three infinitives to complete the sentence: Joan is the right
person ....

g three infinitives to complete the sentence: We must buy
something ....

Vocabulary: Words from the same root

A number of the nouns listed above as frequently being followed by an infinitive are members of the same 'word family' (i.e. they share the same basic root) as verbs which also take the infinitive. For example: The union recorded a *failure to agree* with management. The workers *failed to reach agreement* with the management.

1 Look back at the list of nouns in Grammar Exercise 4 and answer these questions.

a Which of them have a verb from the same root which is also followed by an infinitive?
b What are those verbs?

2 Here is a table with some words from the listening text at the beginning of this unit. The words, however, have been written in the IPA. First translate them into their normal spelling.

Verb(s)	Noun(s)	Adjective(s)	Adverb(s)
ədvaɪz			
	kənsʌmpʃən det		
		liːgəl treɪdɪŋ	
	enədʒi stændəd		

3 Now follow these instructions.

1 Complete the table adding other parts of speech based on the same roots. It may not be possible to fill in all the spaces in the table but some of the spaces can have more than one word. Write the words in their standard spelling not the IPA.

2 Where you find more than one word for a space, explain what the difference is between the different possibilities. For example is one noun abstract and one a person? Is one adjective or adverb positive in meaning and another negative?

4 Choose one of the words from the completed word roots table to complete the gaps in the text below.

It is very difficult to give (1) .... to people who spend too much and so get into (2) .... However, there are a number of different organisations employing (3) .... who do what they can to help. Many of these (4) .... recommend that people should cut down on their (5) .... of food and drink; other organisations give very different suggestions. Needless to say, some organisations tend to give much sounder (6) .... than others. However, it would probably be impossible to (7) .... the recommendations given by different organisations because every (8) ....'s predicament is different. Nevertheless, there should at least be no attempt to act (9) .... in order to extricate themselves from their difficulties; nor, of course, should any attempt to (10) .... on people's misfortune be made by any of the (11) .... organisations. Hopefully, anyone seeking guidance from such an organisation will become (12) .... to them only in a metaphoric sense.

5 Look back at the words from the mail order catalogue text which you matched with their definitions in Reading Exercise 3. Write down another word which has a root in common with each of these words.

Writing: Planning and writing a discursive essay

You are going to write an essay on one of the following topics. They are examples of the kinds of essay subjects which are popular with teachers and examiners in many countries.

- The information super-highway will revolutionise society
- The uses and abuses of junk mail
- It's better to ask advice from people than books
- Useful and useless gadgets

1 When you have to do a piece of writing in any language, it is important to spend some time planning what you are going to say. Do you think it is more important to spend time planning:

a a curriculum vitae or a thank-you letter to a friend?
b an article for a class magazine or an exam essay?
c an advertisement for something you wish to sell or a business memo?

Explain your reasons.

2 Which of these things do you need to bear in mind when planning a piece of writing?

- how to conclude effectively
- how to make an eye-catching opening
- the basic content of what you need or want to say
- the good phrases that you'd like to make use of
- the required length of the piece of writing
- who you are writing for

3 Does your plan for a piece of writing normally look like any of those below? If not, what does it normally look like?

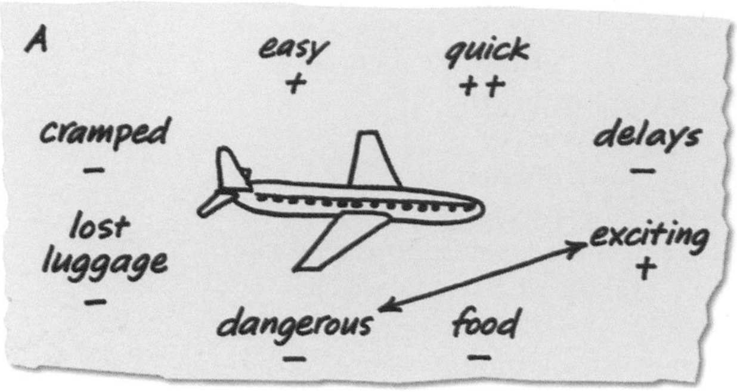

A

easy
+

quick
++

cramped
–

delays
–

lost luggage
–

exciting
+

dangerous
–

food
–

B
1. Intro. Air travel has transformed soc.
2. Advs. of air travel
   speed
   increased business opps.
   Worldwide tourism poss. for all
3. Disadvs. of air travel
   dangerous (sometimes)
   uncomfortable (often)
4. Conclusion Advs. outweigh disadvs.

C

ADVS.	DISADVS.
FAST	DELAYS AIRPORTS LONG WAY FROM TOWNS
CAN SEE WORLD	WORLD BEING DESTROYED BY MASS TOURISM
BREAKFAST IN LONDON, LUNCH IN NEW YORK	→ LUGGAGE IN CAPE TOWN
CAN KEEP IN TOUCH WITH FRIENDS AND RELATIVES AT OTHER SIDE OF THE WORLD	NOWHERE TO ESCAPE TO

4 Discuss with a partner what the advantages are of each of the methods of planning you looked at in Exercise 3.

5 Discursive essays in English tend to follow a fairly standard pattern. Here are some typical plans for approaching a couple of the topics suggested. Each bulleted line in these plans summarises a paragraph of the planned essay.

THE USES AND ABUSES OF JUNK MAIL
• Introduction – what does the term junk mail mean?
• The uses of junk mail:
  a for the sender
  b for the receiver
• The abuses of junk mail:
  a isn't requested and usually isn't wanted
  b is a waste of natural resources
• Conclusion – more abuses than uses

THE INFORMATION SUPER-HIGHWAY WILL REVOLUTIONISE SOCIETY
• Introduction – what does the term information super-highway mean?
• Ways in which it will revolutionise society:
  a broader knowledge of the world
  b contact with machines not people
  c more tele-working (i.e. working from home)
• Ways in which it will not revolutionise society
• Conclusion – yes, on the whole, but not totally

Imagine you were writing the essays and were using the two plans suggested. Which of the following six ideas would it be appropriate to include?

If they can be logically included in the plans outlined, where and how would they fit?

1 The word *super-highway* is a misnomer; it is more like a maze of back streets.
2 Tele-working has important consequences for family life.
3 The machines on which the information super-highway depends are always breaking down.
4 Junk mail is useful for language teachers as material for their students.
5 Junk mail originated in the 18th century.
6 A lot of time and money goes into the preparation of junk mail, so people ought to look at it more carefully.

6 Think about the *Useful and useless gadgets* topic and do the following exercises.

1 As a class brainstorm what you might include in your essay. Don't think about how to order or classify your ideas at this stage. Just say all the ideas that come into your head in the order that they occur to you.
2 In pairs discuss the ideas that have been brainstormed. Which would you use in your essay? Which could be dropped? How might you organise your ideas?
3 Individually, draw up a plan for your essay in any form that seems appropriate for an essay on this subject.
4 Compare the plan you prepared with those of other students in the class.

7 Having the right vocabulary at your finger-tips is an important part of writing an essay in a foreign language. With a partner write down the following (remember to think about verbs and adjectives as well as nouns):

a six words or expressions that could be useful for a discussion of the information super-highway;
b six words or expressions that could be useful when talking about the uses and abuses of junk mail;
c six words or expressions that could be useful when thinking about where to seek advice;
d six words or expressions that could be useful when writing about useful and useless gadgets.

Compare the vocabulary you thought of with the suggestions of other students in the class and write down any other useful words and expressions.

8 Some words and expressions are useful for writing a discursive essay on any topic. Some of these expressions are given in the sentences below in bold but they are incomplete. Can you complete them by adding the missing word? In some cases there may be more than one possible way of filling the blank.

a In this essay **I should first like to** .... **the question** of where the super-highway may be leading society to.
b **I intend to** .... **my essay to** a discussion of the effects of the information revolution on people in my country.
c The answer to this question .... **on how we define** the word *revolutionise*.
d **On the** ...., **I agree with the** .... that the information super-highway will revolutionise society.
e **There are two main** .... **why** I agree with this statement.
f **It cannot be** .... that the person in the street has more access to more information than at any other time in history.
g **It goes without** .... **that** not everyone can take advantage of these opportunities for access to information.
h In the next section of this essay **I should like to** .... **on** the effects of the super-highway on education.
i **Several factors must be taken into** .... when looking at the topic.
j **Let me** .... **my point with the following example**.
k Access to information **has an enormous** .... not only **on** education but also on many other aspects of society.
l Having discussed the effects of the super-highway on young people, **let us now** .... **to a discussion of** how it may affect other groups in society.
m **All things** ...., I remain **firmly in** .... of the information revolution.
n **The advantages** of having greater access to information **far** .... **the disadvantages**.

9 Now choose one of the titles from the beginning of this section and write your essay.

The main aspects of language worked on in this unit are:

- listening to and telling anecdotes
- expressing interest in conversation
- the grammar of the past
- phrasal verbs
- improving your reading speed

Anecdotes are stories which we tell to amuse or entertain our friends. They are often based on our own experience. They often tell people about some particularly frightening, amusing, annoying or curious incident that has happened to the speaker.

Warm-up: Parking stories

You are going to listen to a woman describing what happened to her when she parked her car once in a way which the authorities did not like. First answer these questions.

a What is the law with regard to parking in your country?

b What happens if you park somewhere where you are not supposed to park? What punishment can you be given? How is that punishment exacted? Have you any right of appeal?

c Have you – or has anyone you know – ever had problems with parking (or with some other aspect of driving and the law)? What happened?

d What does the phrase *amusing in retrospect* imply?

Listening: Anecdotes

1 🔊 Listen to the speaker talking about an incident that occurred to her recently. Answer these questions.

a What exactly happened?
b How did she feel at the time?
c How does she feel now?
d How do the friends listening to this anecdote participate? How do they show that they are interested in the story?

2 🔊 Listen to the tape again and read the tapescript on page 168. As you listen, mark any points where you do not understand what the speaker means.

After listening, discuss any of the points you marked with the rest of the class.

Speaking: Expressing interest

1 The three people listening to the parking story expressed their interest in a number of ways. Can you think of any other words and expressions which are often used in English to express interest in what another speaker is saying?

2 ⊟ Listen to the tape. Does the man's voice go up or down in each case?

Now listen again and repeat each exclamation or question after the man. Make your voice go up and down in the same way.

3 With a partner practise reading all the dialogues. Take it in turns to read the roles of A and B.

1 A: I told them they could keep their lousy job.
   B: You didn't!

2 A: Rosie turned up on my doorstep just as I was in the middle of writing her a letter – and we hadn't seen each other or been in touch for nearly five years.
   B: What a coincidence!

3 A: Her boss told her that she either had to marry him or to lose her job.
   B: So what did she do?

4 A: She said she would marry him!
   B: No!

5 A: We're going on holiday to the Caribbean next week!
   B: Mmm?

6 A: The whole holiday only cost £250.
   B: Really?

7 A: My grandmother's maiden name was Day. She married someone called William Week and they had seven children.
   B: How extraordinary!

8 A: I got top marks in all my exams!
   B: Fantastic!

9 A: I should have been at work, I know, but I was really behind with the housework so I called in sick and went off to the supermarket. Who should I bump into as I walked out of the shop but the boss!
   B: Well!

10 A: We'd arranged to meet outside the cinema at seven. I stood there in the cold for two hours but he never turned up.
   B: You stood there for two hours?

4 Answer these questions.

a In dialogue 2, B expresses interest by using *What* + a noun. What are six other nouns which could be used after *What* in this way to express interest?
b In dialogues 7 and 8, B expresses interest by using an adjective. What are six other adjectives which might be used in similar ways to express interest?

5 Work with a partner. Take it in turns to say the extracts from anecdotes below. The other person should respond using as many as possible of the ways of expressing interest practised in Exercises 1 to 4.

a We were sitting on the beach having a picnic in the pouring rain when suddenly we saw something creeping very slowly out of the sea.
b We hadn't met for nearly five years. I got off the train and there he was, waiting for me with a bunch of red roses. I couldn't believe my eyes.
c The examiner told me to go right at the next T-junction. I was just turning when I saw the sign saying 'No right turn'! I stopped automatically and a car behind ran straight into me.
d I suddenly realised that I wasn't sitting on a furry cushion. I was sitting on a little dog.

Grammar: Past tenses

Most stories are told in the past tense – although occasionally in informal speech people use a present tense to add some immediacy to their story. In most cases the particular past tense required to tell a story is the past simple.

You can add interest to a story, both in speaking and writing, by varying the particular past tenses which you use. You could, for instance, set the scene by using the past continuous. Or you could use the past perfect to make the sequencing of events clearer.

The exercises in this section revise and practise the different past tenses in English.

1 Look again at the tapescript of the parking anecdote on page 168 and answer these questions.

a Which different tenses are used in telling the story?
b Which tense is used most frequently?
c When a different tense is used, why do you think it is chosen?

2 Complete the chart.

Name of tense	Form with *do*
past simple	
	was doing
past perfect simple	
	had been doing
	used to do
past conditional	
	have done
present perfect continuous	

Tense	Uses	Examples
past simple		
past continuous		
past perfect		
past conditional		
used to		
present perfect	A	

3 Now look at these uses for the various past tenses. Put the letters in the correct spaces in the chart below left. For example, A should go in the 'Uses' space for the present perfect simple and the present perfect continuous.

A to talk about something which started in the past but is still true now
B to make it clear that something happened before something else in the past
C to talk about past habits
D to talk about something happening at a precise point of time in the past
E to talk about the different events in a story
F to talk about things that did not actually happen but might have done in different circumstances
G to talk about things that happened very recently and have a direct bearing on the present
H to describe the scene around some event that happened
I to describe an action or state in the past interrupted by an event
J to sum up one's experience up to the present time
K to sum up one's experience up to a point of time in the past

Add example sentences (relating to your own experiences during the last few years) for each tense in the appropriate spaces. Write an example to illustrate each of the uses, A–K, summarised above.

4 Here is a story from a newspaper with a number of gaps where verbs are needed. The base forms of the verbs required are provided in brackets. Put each verb into the most appropriate form. Some of the verbs are in a full tense form (mainly one of the past tenses) whereas others are infinitives or gerunds and several others are past participles.

Police (1) .... (hunt) Loch Neuss Monster

Police (2) .... (hunt) Sammy, a fugitive alligator roaming a West German lake, (3) .... (decide) yesterday to bow to pressure and stop (4) .... (try) (5) .... (shoot) it.

The 34-foot-long Cayman (6) .... (gain) a fan club since it (7) .... (slip) its leash on a hot Saturday and (8) .... (slither) into the lake at a bathing resort not far from the town of Neuss. The police who (9) .... (hunt) Sammy with rifles from pedal-boats and dinghies, (10) .... (use) blood-stained steak as bait, (11) .... (say) yesterday that they (12) .... (try) (13) .... (catch) it alive. 'We (14) .... (overwhelm) by sympathy for Sammy.'

Last week, hundreds of bathers (15) .... (enjoy) the waters of the lake when Sammy (16) .... (flee) from his owner, 21-year-old Jorg Zars, and (17) .... (slide) into the cooling water (18) .... (escape) a searing heatwave. 'It (19) .... (be) really tame,' (20) .... (say) Herr Zars. 'It (21) .... (sleep) in my bed at night before it (22) .... (grow) so large.' But experts say the Cayman – (23) .... (dub) the Loch Neuss Monster by the media – can rip through flesh like a shark with his razor-sharp teeth. The resort, (24) .... (force) (25) .... (shut down) during the heatwave while police (26) .... (search) for Sammy (27) .... (lose) thousands of pounds. If it (28) .... (not be) for Sammy's escape, the

waters of the lake (29) .... (be) crowded with bathers on these boiling days.

By yesterday the alligator (30) .... (became) a hero with its own fan club, (31) .... (set up) by the Saarland radio station whose switchboard (32) .... (jam) by listeners (33) .... (call) in with messages of sympathy. 'By ten o'clock last night we (34) .... (receive) over one thousand calls.'

Vocabulary: Phrasal verbs

Phrasal verbs are frequently used in English. Although they are particularly common in conversation and in popular journalism, they can also be found in more serious writing and more formal speech.

1 What are the three examples of phrasal verbs used in the Loch Neuss Monster article?

2 Look at these sentences which show some characteristic uses of phrasal verbs. Underline the phrasal verb in each case.

Write one word which might be used to replace the phrasal verb if the same idea were being described in a piece of formal writing.

a We'd been expecting a large audience but only about fifteen people turned up for the lecture. It was very disappointing.

b I could never get any work done in such a small noisy office. And it's not as if they pay you a lot to compensate. I can't understand why you put up with such dreadful conditions.

c Come and look out of the window. Something's going on in the street. But there's such a crowd it's hard to make out what's actually happening. Can you see what it is?

d It's about two hundred miles from here to York, but the roads are quite fast. If we set off at midday, we should easily get there by teatime.

e We've just bought a house on Rosamund Street. It was relatively cheap, but it needs a lot of work on it. We're doing it up a bit before we move in.

f He's got such a nice manner that a lot of normally sensible people have been quite taken in by him. Even Sally believed everything he told her and she's normally on the ball.

g The wonderful situation of the hotel and its beautiful rooms certainly made up for rather inferior food. We might well stay there next year but we'd just book bed and breakfast another time.

h This job is really beginning to get us all down. We've been working on it for so long and we still don't seem to have made any progress with it.

i There have been far too many road accidents at the corner of Coronation Street and Ramsey Street. It's time they held an enquiry to look into the situation. They've been talking about doing something for ages.

j He loves playing practical jokes but somehow they never quite come off. Like the time he put a drawing pin on the teacher's seat and then forgot about it and sat on it himself!

3 Work with a partner and a dictionary. Follow these instructions.

1 Take one of these verbs – your teacher will tell you which verb your pair should work on.

> see   break   run   catch   work   tell   talk   try

2 Look in the dictionary to see how many phrasal verbs based on this verb you can find.

3 Write these verbs down in the way that you find most helpful for learning them. You might, for example, find a ripple diagram useful.

4 Decide which two of the verbs you found would be most useful for the other students in your class to know. Teach those verbs to the other students.

A

let   turn
look   come
take   go   make
put   do   set
get   bring

B

across
after   at
back   by   down
in   off   on
out   through
up

4 Work with a partner. Look at the verbs in circle A and the prepositions or particles in circle B. In five minutes write down as many phrasal verbs as you can (there are at least 150!) in example sentences. Notice that one combination may make more than one phrasal verb, e.g. *Fifty people turned up at the party; Please turn up the radio; This dress is too long. I must turn it up*, etc. Each different meaning counts as a different verb.

5 Follow the instructions to play a phrasal verb game.

1 Play in groups of four to six people. Sit in a circle.
2 Write all the verbs in Exercise 4 on slips of paper, shuffle them and put them face down in a pile.
3 Write all the prepositions/particles in Exercise 4 on slips of paper, shuffle them and put them face down in a pile.
4 Take it in turns to play clockwise round the circle.
5 Each player in turn turns over the papers at the top of the verb and the preposition piles. If that player can make a correct sentence using that verb and that preposition in one minute, then he or she is still in the game. If the player cannot do so – and someone else in the group can – then he or she is out. If no one else can either, then the player can exchange either the verb or the preposition card and have another try. This can continue until either the player finds a good sentence or is out.
6 The next player turns over the next verb and preposition and play continues in the same way. The last player to be out is the winner.
7 When all the slips of paper from each pile have been used, then they are shuffled and placed face down again before the game continues.
8 Players who are already out may challenge if they think that someone suggests a sentence that is not correct. If their challenge is passed by a teacher or a dictionary, then they are back in the game.

Speaking: Telling anecdotes

Read all the instructions before you start doing the exercise.

1 Sit with a group of three or four other students.
2 Imagine that you are in a café or somewhere else together telling stories.
3 Your teacher will give you some ideas to tell to the other people. Take it in turns to tell a story.
4 When you are listening to other people's stories, make sure that you show your interest by using appropriate exclamations, questions and interjections.
5 When one person's story comes to an end, someone else should begin with one of theirs. But try to carry on in a natural conversational way. The next person might, for example, use a linking phrase like one of the following:
That reminds me of when …
That's nothing compared to the time …
I must tell you about …
Did I ever tell you about …?
Something a bit like that happened to me when …
A funny thing happened to me yesterday …
6 Before you start, spend a few minutes – but not too long – thinking about which story (or stories) you could tell.
7 Begin when all the students in your group are ready.

Study skills: Improve your reading speed

Whether you are reading an ephemeral newspaper story like the one about the alligator in Lake Neuss or something that is important for your work, you will save yourself a lot of time if you can improve your reading speed. The technique for doing this which is introduced below – and practised further in Unit 21 – will help your reading in both your own language and in English.

1 Start reading the article. Stop after one minute. Estimate the number of words you have read – there are 504 in all in the article. Make a note of that number.

2 In the article, the world renowned psychologist, Tony Buzan, uses the term *fixation*. In this context, *fixation* means the pauses made by our eyes as we read. We *fixate* in order to assimilate the next groups of words to be read. Read the text and make notes of the key points which Buzan makes.

One advantage for the faster reader is that his eye will be doing less physical work on each page. Rather than having as many as 500 fixations tightly focused per page as does the slow reader, he will have as few as 100 fixations per page, each one of which is less muscularly fatiguing. Another advantage is that the rhythm and flow of the faster reader will carry him comfortably through the meaning, whereas the slow reader, because of his stopping and starting, jerky approach, will be far more likely to become bored, to lose concentration, to mentally drift away and to lose the meaning of what he is reading.

It is clear that a number of commonly held myths about faster reading are false:

Words must be read one at a time:

Wrong. Because of our ability to fixate and because we read for meaning rather than for single words.

Reading faster than 500 wpm is impossible:

Wrong. Because the fact that we can take in as many as six words per fixation and the fact that we can make four fixations a second means that speeds of 1,000 wpm are perfectly feasible.

The faster reader is not able to appreciate:

Wrong. Because the faster reader will be understanding more of the meaning of what he reads, he will be concentrating on the material more and will have considerably more time to go back over areas of special interest and importance to him.

Higher speeds give lower concentration:

Wrong. Because the faster we go, the more impetus we gather and the more we concentrate.

Average reading speeds are natural and therefore the best:

Wrong. Because average reading speeds are not natural. They are speeds produced by an incorrect initial training in reading, combined with an inadequate knowledge of how the eye and brain work at the various speeds possible.

Most reading is done at a relaxed and almost lackadaisical pace, a fact of which many speed reading courses have taken advantage. Students are given various exercises and tasks and it is suggested to them that after each exercise their speed will increase by 10–20 wpm. And so it does, often by as much as 100 per cent over the duration of the lessons. The increase, however, is often due, not to the exercises, but to the fact that the student's motivation has often been eked out bit by bit during the course. The same significant increases could be produced by guaranteeing each student at the beginning of the course the fulfilment of any wish he desired. Performance would immediately equal that normally achieved at the end of such courses – similar to the unathletic fellow who runs 100 metres in ten seconds flat and jumps a six-foot fence when being chased by a bull. In these cases, motivation is the major factor, and the reader will benefit enormously by consciously applying it to each learning experience. If a deep-rooted decision is made to do better, then poor performance will automatically improve.

3 Now see if your reading speed has increased. Read the anecdote below for one minute and count the number of words you have read. Note the number. Was it more than the number you managed in Exercise 1?

A few years back a friend studying at Brunel University was lucky enough to grab a seat in a packed lecture hall to hear an address given by an eminent professor to the university's engineering society. The don was delivering an oration on the subject of unusual railway bridges so, as you would expect, the hall was full to bursting with budding engineers and their peers. The learned professor cut a fine figure at the lectern and, well practised in the art of public speaking, punctuated his talk with pithy comments and slides of the breathtaking constructions. His knowledge seemed to know no bounds: he knew his subject inside out. He singled out many interesting and innovative designs for praise, dropping names like 'aitches' at a cockney knees-up, then turned on one particularly unusual example and slated it. He criticised the titanic structure's size, the design, the construction methods and the impact on the environment. He did not like that bridge!

When the applause had died down, there was a question and answer session. An elderly gentleman raised his hand and, returning to the subject of the maligned bridge, took some time to explain the reasons, as he understood them, for the unusual nature of the bridge's aspect and fabrication.

The professor, his feathers ruffled by this contentious interruption and feeling the limelight slipping away, puffed out his chest and pointedly put the old fellow down for audaciously implying that he knew more about the subject than the professor did himself.

'Well, I should,' replied the studious old fellow. 'You see, I designed and built that particular bridge myself.'

4 Remember the points which Buzan makes when you read, both in your own language and in English. The ability to read faster can be a useful life skill.

9 Gifts from the boss
Business articles

The main aspects of language worked on in this unit are:

- reading business articles
- weak forms in speech
- singulars and plurals
- the vocabulary of business English
- collecting and using articles

Warm-up: Job satisfaction

Follow these instructions.

1 List five things which, for you, would be essential ingredients for job satisfaction, e.g. opportunities to travel, working outdoors, doing something creative, a good salary, a clear routine.

2 List three things which, for you, would be particularly negative things in a job, e.g. shift work, having to wear a uniform, working on your own.

3 How far does your own current or planned job match your likes and dislikes?

4 Exchange your lists with those of other students. Suggest some jobs which would seem to suit the various lists of likes and dislikes. What do the students involved think about your suggestions for them?

5 The text you are going to read is about one way for companies to reward good work. What methods of rewarding good work have you experienced or heard of?

Reading: PRGs

1 Look at the pictures. What do they suggest about the content of the text?

2 Read the text and summarise what the article is about in one sentence.

GIVING IT

AWAY

Is the gold-plated carriage clock making a comeback? Having spent the 1980s inventing ever more sophisticated forms of performance-related pay (PRP), businesses are rediscovering the merits of a rather older way of motivating people: performance-related gifts (PRGs). Firms as diverse as Marlow Industries, an American manufacturer of thermo-electric coolers, the Automobile Association, a British club which helps motorists whose cars break down, and Barclays, a British bank, are using presents, from Caribbean cruises to colour televisions, to reward outstanding work. This is a bit of a surprise to management theorists who used to dismiss PRGs as relics of a bygone era of exorbitant tax rates and corporate paternalism. Why should British managers waste their time thinking up gifts when a decade of tax reforms has done away with the need to bribe employees with company cars and subsidised lunches? Why should American firms bother with baubles when flexible pay systems are supposed to reward good performance? In countries such as Japan, where top tax rates exceed 90% and promotion depends on seniority, companies might have to show their appreciation with foreign holidays and golf-club memberships; in a growing number of Western countries, companies could surely just pay people what they are worth.

In fact, paying people what they are worth is not always enough. Having fallen in love with performance-related pay in the 1980s, many managers are turning against it,

complaining that it is expensive (salaries tend to flex up not down), clumsy (in many areas, people cannot agree on how to define good performance) and demoralising (the winners are encouraged only briefly, while the losers fall into a permanent sulk). Gifts, on the other hand, seem to allow a show of appreciation for one person's outstanding work without annoying everyone else. And they are usually pretty cheap. Consider Avon Products, an American direct sales company specialising in beauty products. In 1992 the company's North American divisions tried to give up in-house prizes: reducing travel awards, cutting commissions and stopping the practice of sending birthday presents to high performers. Avon had long rewarded its sales people with points which could be traded for gifts; now it insisted that the points could be used only to buy savings bonds.

The result was widespread anger and hostility among the company's crack force of 400,000 'Avon ladies' who sell beauty products door to door. Christina Gold, who took over as head of Avon's American, Canadian and

Puerto Rican operations in November 1993, immediately set about reintroducing the in-house prizes. She has cut expenditure on brochures and ploughed the money saved into sales incentives, put together a new catalogue of gifts, and instructed her managers to send hand-written thank-you letters to their Avon ladies.

Other companies are embracing the gift-giving habit. Levi Strauss, a leisurewear firm, gives everyone at its San Francisco headquarters a small number of 'You Are Great' coupons, which they can hand out to any of their colleagues doing a particularly good job. Recipients can trade in the coupons for $25 or a gift certificate, or else frame them and display them on their desks. Department heads each have a budget, which they can use to give spur-of-the-moment rewards worth up to $150 (e.g. a ticket to the big game). To cap it all, each division regularly holds formal events, where employees, spouses and friends gather to hand out 'personal hero' awards to top performers.

American firms are not alone in discovering the power of PRGs. For the past two years, Whitbread Inns, a division of Whitbread, a British brewer, has run a 'share in success' scheme. Bar staff who hit their monthly sales targets, or complete a recognised training programme, are rewarded with credits which they can use to buy gifts – ranging from wrist watches to balloon trips – from a catalogue. The firm also provides managers with a fistful of extra credits, which they dole out to publicans who greet their customers with a particularly affable smile.

---

3 Answer the following questions.

a What are PRGs?
b Make a list of all the PRGs mentioned in the article.
c Can you find them all in the illustrations on the previous page?
d What is PRP?

e Why are people not so enthusiastic as they used to be about PRP?
f What are the advantages of PRGs over PRP?
g Have you – or has anyone you know – ever received a PRG?
h How would you feel if you were offered one?
i Which of the gifts mentioned in the article would you (a) like (b) not like to be offered?

Speaking: Weak forms

In Unit 3, we saw how important stress is in both words and sentences in English. Syllables that are not stressed are pronounced in a very weak way in English. It sometimes seems as if English people swallow half their words. The most common vowel sound in English is the schwa (ə) or unstressed vowel. The schwa sound is not associated with any particular written letter or combination of letters; *a, e, i, o* and *u* and any combinations of those letters can all be pronounced as schwa when they are in an unstressed position.

If you want to sound natural in English, then you must be careful not to pronounce unstressed words or syllables too fully.

1 Follow these instructions.

1 ▭ Listen to the text and take it down as dictation.
2 Underline all the stressed syllables.
3 Decide which of the unstressed words and syllables contain a schwa sound.
4 Read the text, taking care not to over-stress any words or syllables which should not carry a stress.

2 What kinds of words do you think are usually unstressed when we speak?

3 Think of example sentences where the speaker might want to stress

a the article *the*;
b the preposition *of*;
c the auxiliary verb *do*.

4 ▭ A number of structural words in English – like *the, of* and *do* – have very different pronunciations depending on whether they are stressed or not.

Look at the italicised words in the sentences in the box below. Listen to the sentence being pronounced in two different ways – the first is the normal pronunciation of the sentence; the second has the italicised word stressed because the speaker wishes to give it a special emphasis in the particular context.

Notice what happens to the pronunciation of the italicised words. Write them down in IPA for both pronunciations.

> I *was* first.   We *could* help.
> *Do* you know her?   We *must* go.
> Can I have *some* help?
> They asked *us* to wait.   He flew *to* Paris.
> Look at *the* man.
> They've got a cat *and* a dog.   I'll *be* there.
> He *will* be late.   Give me *your* book.

5 Practise saying each sentence in the two different ways.

6 Here are some dialogues which would encourage the speaker to stress some of the sentences in the way indicated in the box.

In each case why is it appropriate to stress a word that would normally not be stressed?

Read the dialogues, with the appropriate stresses.

A: I'm sure you couldn't have come first – not out of a class of forty.
B: I *was* first. I knew you'd be surprised.

A: I don't really want to help him write his dissertation, do you?
B: No, I don't but I feel a bit mean because I know we *could* help. We know far more about how to present a dissertation than he does.

A: Is that the girl we were talking about last night?
B: Yes, that's right. The one that I thought you knew but you swore you didn't. *Do* you know her?

7 With a partner write dialogues to illustrate how the other sentences in the box might occur in a natural way.

Practise reading your dialogues.

8 Read this text of a business news announcement.

> STERLING today is steady against the dollar but is down sharply against the deutsch mark. The dollar is up against the yen. This has caused some movement on the Tokyo Stock Market which closed 22 points down. Now for some other headlines from today's business news. Almost half of the workers who left their jobs last year had been employed for more than five years. The latest survey from the Employment Research Council reports that the highest staff turnover is among those employed in retailing and part-timers.
>
> Pay increases over the last six months have been holding steady. Increases from the period April to September averaged three and a half per cent, which is virtually the same as the equivalent figure for the same period last year.
>
> Spending on tourism this summer topped four billion pounds, a record high. The most popular fee-charging destination for tourists was Alton Towers, which has already attracted five million visitors this year. The most popular tourist destination of all is the British Museum, which is free, and this has already had six million visitors this year.

Which words/syllables would you expect to be stressed when the news broadcast is read aloud?

9 ⬛ Listen to a newscaster reading this news broadcast and underline the words which the speaker stresses.

Listen again and draw lines to mark the points where the speaker pauses.

10 ⬛ Now listen to the tape and repeat each section in the space provided after each pause.

11 ⬛ Listen to the first reading of the complete news broadcast again and try to speak with the speaker. Take care that you stress only the words that the speaker stresses. Do not give extra stress to other words or you will soon get out of step with the speaker.

Vocabulary: Business English

1 Read through the article about PRGs again and underline all the words and expressions in it which relate specifically to business, e.g. performance-related pay.

2 Among the words and expressions which you have underlined, can you find words or expressions that mean:

a presents given to workers who work particularly well;
b people who work for a company;
c being given a better job within a company;
d length of service in a particular company;
e amount of money paid to a sales person depending on how much he or she actually sells;
f the main office of a company or organisation;
g people who work together in the same company or profession;
h to achieve plans for quantities to be sold.

3 Divide all the words and expressions that you underlined in the article into groups. Group them in any way that you feel will help you to learn the words. You might, for instance, want to use some of the following categories, but feel free to choose quite different categories if you prefer:

people   organisations   money   incentives

4 Underline any useful business words in the text of the news broadcast. Fit these into the categories which you identified in Exercise 3. Make any new categories necessary.

5 Compare the way you categorised the words with the system used by another student.

Looking at both your systems, can you find two or three more business-related words or expressions which you could add to each of the categories you used? If you cannot think of anything, ask another pair of students, or the teacher, to help you.

6 You are going to read another business article. It contains a lot of typical business words but these have been taken out. They are in the box below.

acquired   acquisitions   components   demand   dividend industry   loss   manufacturer   profits   share   trebled turnover

Before you read the article, match the words in the box to the definitions below. (Sometimes more than one meaning is possible but the ones used in the definition refer to the words as they will be used in the text which follows.)

a amount of money handled by a company in a specific period of time
b amount of money paid regularly to share-holders (investors) in a company
c companies taken over
d desire for a particular product
e grew three times as large
f money earned in a business after paying costs
g money lost in a business after paying costs
h one equal part of the ownership of a company which can be bought by members of the public
i one type of business
j parts
k producer of goods in large numbers
l purchased

7 Read the article. Can you put the words back in the correct places?

Restructured Rubicon Up 84%

Rubicon Group, which in a series of (1) .... and sales has been transformed from a shop equipment business into a precision engineering group, yesterday reported an 84 per cent advance in pre-tax (2) .... for the year to May 31.

The increase, from £1.22m to £2.35m, was achieved on turnover almost (3) .... from £18.1m to £50m. Earnings per (4) .... came out at 9.1p (7.5p) and a recommended final (5) .... of 2.8p makes a total for the year of 4.6p (4p).

The improvement was principally the result of a strong contribution from High Speed Production, a (6) .... of precision (7) .... and assemblies for the electronics (8) ...., (9) .... for £9m in July last year.

At the year end, the shop equipment businesses were sold. These operations had been suffering from weak (10) ...., directors said, and had incurred an operating (11) .... of £160,000 on (12) .... of £20.4m.

Grammar: Singular and plural

On the whole, singular and plural, often referred to grammatically as *number*, is not too big a problem in English – you don't have a lot of irregular plurals to learn, for example. But there are some aspects of the grammar of *number* which can cause difficulty.

1 Try this quiz in teams to see how 'numerate' you are.

Number Quiz

1 Do these words need a singular or a plural verb – everyone, everybody, everything?

2 Do these words need a singular or a plural verb?
a people; police; cattle
b family; team; government; committee; school; staff; council; choir; firm; company
c news; measles; the United States; draughts (the game)

3 What are the plural forms of these nouns?

appendix (in a book) phenomenon tooth goose formula mouse louse curriculum radius fungus sheep deer fish mother-in-law child aircraft criterion basis crisis thesis hypothesis index (e.g. economic) man woman person

Now count up your score.

Give yourselves 3 marks for a correct answer to question 1 and each of the three parts of question 2 and 1 mark for each correct plural in question 3.

Which team is the winner?

2 How do you say the singular and plural forms of these words?

> woman   basis   crisis   hypothesis   index
> appendix

Practise pronouncing both forms. You may find it helps you to write each word in both its singular and plural forms in the IPA (using a dictionary if necessary).

3 Follow these instructions.

1 Choose five words that you particularly want to use from the quiz and write sentences using those words.
2 Read one of your sentences to a partner but do not say the word you are trying to learn – just say *blob* instead. For example, *I find it very hard to learn mathematical blobs by heart.* Your partner must try to guess what *blob* stands for!
3 Take it in turns to work through all your sentences in this way.

Study skills: Collecting and using articles

Pizzas on Antarctic trek

THERE'S nothing unusual in ringing a delivery company for six large pizzas — bu... ...es from Scott Base, Antarctica.

Eagle Boys Dia... order for six larg... Scott Base, and ... claims that the e... the longest in th...

How museums are turning us into old fossils

MUSEUMS might improve the mind but they can leave you feeling like a relic.

Hours of trudging along endless corridors and peering into display cases

by SIMON YOUNG

half miles of corridors and several million items."

Many museums have made efforts to reduce the

It can be useful and interesting to cut out and keep newspaper or magazine articles which you find interesting. You could simply put them in a scrapbook or you could use them for exercises to do on your own or with other students.

Try these two exercises to give you some idea of the sorts of things you might do with articles which you collect. The first one is to be done with another student, the second can be done either alone or with others.

1 Follow these instructions.

1 Bring to class an article that interests you.
2 Write six to ten questions on the article. Try to write questions that you would like to know the answers to. For example, you might want to ask about the meaning of a word or phrase that you are not sure of, you might want to ask a question to check whether you have really understood the gist of what the writer is saying, or you might want to find out what another student's opinion is of some point made in the article.
3 Exchange articles and questions with another student. Read that student's article and discuss how to answer his or her questions on the article.

2 Follow these instructions.

1 Choose an article that interests you. Read through the article and cover up some of the words in it (by using correcting fluid, for example). *Make sure, however, that you keep a note of which words you covered.* If it is possible to keep a photocopy of the complete article, that would be very convenient.
2 It is important to cover words which can be discovered from the context. Suitable words may be prepositions, articles, pronouns, words from fixed expressions and so on.
3 Now look back at your article. Can you remember / work out what the missing words are?
4 Keep the article – and the Key! A week or two weeks later, try this exercise again.
5 You can, of course, do this exercise with a partner, testing each other with the articles you have prepared.

I can't agree with you!
Giving opinions

10

The main aspects of language worked on in this unit are:

- listening to and giving opinions
- questions and answers
- discourse markers
- giving a talk

Warm-up: Giving opinions

Work in pairs and follow these instructions.

1 Write down three topics that you feel strongly about – for example, a social issue, a particular film or musical group, something that has happened recently.

2 Show your list of three topics to your partner and ask him or her to choose one of them.

3 Give your opinion on that topic to your partner. Try to speak for at least a minute. Then ask your partner if he or she shares your point of view.

4 Spend another minute discussing your topic together.

5 Follow the same procedure with you choosing one of your partner's topics.

Listening: Giving opinions

1 ▭ **Listen to the tape and note down answers to the following questions.**

a How many people are talking?

b What topic are they discussing?

c What is the basic point of view of each of them?

Compare your answers with those of other students in the class.

2 ☐ Listen to the tape again. Listen particularly to one of the speakers – your teacher will tell you which one to focus on. Make notes in answer to these questions.

a How well does your speaker put across his or her opinion? Do you agree with him or her?

b Does your speaker make any particularly effective uses of stress and intonation?

c Does your speaker use any good general phrases for discussing and putting across an opinion, e.g. *I think; I'm sorry, I can't agree with you.*

d What kind of person do you think your speaker is?

Compare your answers with those of other students in the class.

3 How well do you think the people who were discussing women and work in the previous exercise know each other? Look at the tapescript on pages 169–70 and base your answer on the way they spoke to each other.

4 Read this extract from what they said to each other and answer the questions below.

CHRIS: Having a family is not simple, it's not a little bag that you carry around with you, it's an enormous job, it's two jobs in fact. That and work. So why can't a man take on the two jobs?

JANE: Absolutely.

DAVID: I think a man does take on the two jobs. (*Laughter*)

CHRIS: Rubbish.

a How does Jane show her agreement with Chris and how does Chris show his disagreement with David?

b How formal or informal are these ways of agreeing and disagreeing?

c If the situation had been much more formal (for example, a discussion between people of very different ages who did not know each other well), how might Jane and Chris have expressed their agreement and disagreement?

d If the situation had been much less formal (for example, a group of teenagers who had been to school together for the last five years), how might Jane and Chris have expressed their agreement and disagreement?

5 Can you think of ten more good phrases for giving opinions to add to those used by the speakers on the tape?

Divide your list of expressions into formal and informal.

Grammar: Questions and answers

1 Questions are used a great deal when opinions are being discussed. Look at the tapescript of the discussion you listened to (on pages 169–70) and follow these instructions.

1 Underline or highlight all the questions in it.

2 Find an example in the tapescript of each of these types of questions:

a one asked in order to check whether another person agrees with the speaker;

b one asked in order to get more information about something another speaker has mentioned;

c one asked with the intention of finding out another person's opinion on a subject (when you really have no idea what that opinion might be);

d one that is purely rhetorical (i.e. asked just to make a forceful statement and not expecting any answer to be given);

e one that is asked in order to take the discussion on a stage.

2 Imagine you were taking part in the discussion which you listened to on the tape. Think of two more questions which you could have inserted into the conversation. What would your questions have been, and at what points in the discussion might you have asked them?

3 Here are some common question words. Match them with their answers.

Where?	Just because.
Who?	To see the manager.
When?	Very nice.
Why?	Last week.
Whose?	Ten pounds.
Which?	At home.
How long?	Two years.
How much?	In ten days.
How many?	Medium.
How soon?	Circular.
How old?	A dozen.
What ... like?	Mine.
What ... for?	Jane.
What shape?	Ten.
What size?	This one.

4 What questions might someone have asked to receive the following answers?

a I just wanted to see what would happen if I mixed the two chemicals together.

b Why don't you leave him and go and get a job abroad?

c I'll be wearing a rose in my buttonhole and carrying a copy of *The Financial Times*.

d It was a bit of a disappointment really. They sound much better on disc.

e Take the 31 bus and get off at the stop after the bridge. We're just round the corner from the bus stop.

f Absolutely fantastic. It didn't rain once.

g I'm just trying to get it working.

h Not really. I've got used to it now.

i No, I wouldn't. I think it's high time we had a change.

j Not bad, she can be a bit of a slave driver but she's basically fair, I suppose.

5 Look at these sentences.

It's a lovely day, isn't it?
You met her parents, didn't you?
You haven't been to Australia, have you?
You can't play bridge, can you?

In informal speech, we often use tag questions to invite a response. Note that we normally expect the person to agree with us. Are there any examples of tag questions in the discussion you listened to on tape?

6 Complete these basic rules for the formation of question tags.

1 If the statement is positive, the tag question is
....

2 If the statement is negative, the tag question is
....

3 The tag question uses an .... verb which matches the main verb in the statement.

4 If the main verb in the statement is in the present simple, the verb in the tag will be
....

5 If the main verb in the statement is in the past simple, the verb in the tag will be
....

6 If the main verb in the statement is in the past continuous form, then the verb in the tag will be ....

7 If the main verb in the statement is in the present perfect form, then the verb in the tag will be ....

8 If the main verb in the statement contains a modal verb, then the verb in the tag will be
....

9 The subject of the tag is the .... which relates to the subject of the main statement.

10 So, if the subject of the main statement is *Charles and Priscilla*, then the subject of the tag will be ....

11 If the subject of the main statement is *the weather* then the subject of the tag question will be ....

12 If the subject of the main statement is a pronoun, then the subject of the tag will be
....

7 There are, however, a few exceptions to these rules. Examples of the exceptions are all provided in the sentences below – though there are some ordinary examples too.

Add the necessary tag questions to these statements.

a I'm not too bossy, ...
b I'm being bossy, ...
c Nobody likes him very much, ...
d Anyone can learn English, ...
e Something will turn up, ...
f There's a problem here, ...
g This is the problem, ...
h Don't ever forget me, ...
i Open the door for me, ...
j Do sit here, ...
k The baby's asleep, ...
l The dog's been fed, ...
m Bill must work hard, ...
n Jill had to work hard, ...
o If we arrive early, we can have a cup of coffee at that place beside the station, ...
p You used to play championship tennis, ...
q Diana'd rather not go out tonight, ...
r Tom'd better stay at home too, ...
s We may pay by credit card, ...
t Jane needs to bring her own tennis racket, ...

8 What do the examples of tag questions in Exercise 7 show us about the following?

a the way *I am* in the main statement is transformed into a tag;
b the pronoun which relates to *someone, no one, everybody, anyone*, etc.;
c the pronoun which relates to *thing* compounds (*something*, etc.);
d the gender of babies and animals in English;
e what *'d* in *'d better* and *'d rather* is short for.

9 Asking questions about language is especially important for students of English. Can you ask the following questions accurately?

a Ask about the meaning of these words and expressions – *to deteriorate, to look at life through rose-tinted glasses, a charity, adoption*.
b Ask about the pronunciation of these place names – *Edinburgh, Leicester*
c Ask about the spelling of these words: əkɒmədeɪʃən   ɪgzɪləreɪtɪŋ

10 A lot of games are based on questions and answers and so are a good way of practising this important aspect of language. The 'What Am I?' game is one example.

▭ Listen to the instructions for this game on the tape. Check that the instructions are clear and then play the game.

11 Do you know any other question and answer games? Explain the rules to the class and then play the game.

12 ▭ Journalists ask a lot of questions but sometimes their job is quite difficult. Listen to this radio reporter interviewing an old man who has been selected to take part in an athletics competition and answer these questions.

a What questions does he ask the old man?
b What do listeners learn about the old man?
c Could the interviewer have handled the situation better?

13 Play another question game by following these instructions.

1 As a class, brainstorm the names of about six famous people from the past whom you would like to meet. Write their names on the board.

2 Individually, write down ten questions which you would like to ask one or more of these people. You may prepare all your questions for one person or five for one person and five for another – or they may be for six different people, if you prefer. Try to think of questions which would be likely to lead to interesting answers.

3 Compare the questions you wrote with those prepared by other students in the class. Explain why you felt you would like to ask these particular questions.

4 Choose one person in the class to play one of the characters you chose. Ask him or her your questions.

Vocabulary: Discourse markers

Discourse markers are small words or phrases which serve to clarify the organisation of what we are saying or writing.

The speakers on the taped discussion at the beginning of this unit use a number of expressions which English people frequently use when they speak, but which do not have much meaning. They are words or phrases like *I mean* or *basically*; although they do not convey much meaning, they are helpful when we speak because they allow us a bit more time to organise our thoughts and try to put them into words.

1 ▭ Listen again to the conversation you listened to at the beginning of this unit and note down any words and expressions that seem to you to have this time-gaining function rather than being used to convey meaning.

2 Here are some discourse markers which are characteristic of spoken English. Frequently they serve the purpose of allowing the speaker time to think. Sometimes, however, their purpose is to attract someone's attention. Look at the list and answer the questions below.

well	now then	listen	mind you	you know	kind of
sort of	you see	anyway	look here	I mean	I think
I'd say	basically	really	actually	of course	let me think
let's see	so to speak	like

a Which of the speech discourse markers in the list above do you think are used mainly to allow time to think?

b Which do you think are used mainly to attract the listeners' attention?

c Can you suggest any other ways of giving yourself time to organise your thoughts when you are speaking English?

3 Read the following text and answer these questions about it.

  a What is the person in the monologue doing as he speaks?
  b Who is he speaking to?
  c Why is very little punctuation used?
  d What kind of discourse markers are used and why are they used?
  e Would what is being said be clearer if more discourse markers were used? If so, what could be added and where could they be added?

> …ha ha ha that's very good er apparently this chap held up a grocery store and they thought he er had a gun but actually it was a sausage and the funny thing was the man's name was Mr Banger ha ha ha … listen to this an old lady of 95 was mugged in her own home oh dear oh dear what sort of society are we living in? this is interesting there's a new EC regulation that says you can't sell cheese in a tobacconist what will they think of next? I ask you … oh they're doing a boules set for £53.45 with its own travelling bag do you remember that village we stopped off in Provence where the old men were playing? what was it called? who is this Hurley girl whose picture is in every day? wasn't she in some film? there's a story here about a hen in China that's laid 8 million eggs I don't believe it they'll put anything in the papers nowadays … oh dear poor old Quentin Felchett has died only 72 you remember him? he was the vicar in what was it the one with Alastair Sim … oh look Norman's niece Jenny and Mark have had a little girl called Tabitha will you send a card? I'm not disturbing you am I? …

4 Follow these instructions.

  1 Take a slip of paper and write on it a topic that you think other students in the class might find rather difficult (but not impossible) to talk about for a minute – for example, camels, cutting your nails, going to the butcher's, lawn mowers.
  2 Shuffle the slips of paper.
  3 Take it in turns to take a piece of paper and attempt to speak for a minute on that subject. You should try to leave no silences but to fill your thinking pauses with some of the discourse markers in the list in Exercise 2.
  4 Decide as a class which three students managed to do this most successfully.

Speaking: Giving a talk

Some talks are interesting to listen to, whereas we find it hard to concentrate during others or find it hard to understand what the speaker is trying to say.

1 Answer the following questions, thinking about talks in your own language as well as talks in English. Brainstorm as many ideas as you can and write them in two columns on the board – Good characteristics and Bad characteristics of a talk.

  a What makes a talk interesting?
  b What makes a talk dull and difficult to follow?

2 ☐ Listen to the advice on the tape about making a talk interesting and answer these questions.

a How many of the points mentioned on the tape did you think of yourselves?
b Did you think of any points which were not mentioned on the tape?

3 You are going to prepare a talk to give to the class. Follow these instructions.

1 Choose one of the topics in the box. You can argue either for or against the statement in your talk.

> Men and women are good at different things.
> Euthanasia can sometimes be justified.
> The best things in life are free.
> No sane person would want to become a politician.
> Smoking should be banned in all public places.
> Parents should be prevented by law from smacking their children.
> Schooldays are the happiest days of your life.
> Work is the opium of people today.
> Animals are nicer than people.
> Love is blind.

If you prefer you may choose some other topic that you have a strong opinion on.
2 Prepare notes for a five-minute talk to the class. Bear in mind the good and bad characteristics of a talk discussed in Exercises 1 and 2.
3 Give your talk to the class.

After each student's talk, the rest of the class should ask questions on the content of the talk and give feedback on the presentation of the talk.

The main aspects of language worked on in this unit are:
- reading magazine articles
- the grammar of modals
- register
- writing a report

Warm-up: Reading magazines

Answer the following questions.

a Which magazines do you read (a) regularly and (b) occasionally in your own language?

b What sorts of articles can you find in the magazines that you read in your own language?

c What sorts of articles do you (a) enjoy and (b) not particularly enjoy reading?

d Are there similar magazines in English to those you regularly or occasionally read in your own language?

e Below are the titles of some magazines in English. What sorts of magazines do you think they are? What kind of articles would you expect to find in them? In what ways do you think the register in these magazines might differ?

Reading: The good old days?

1 Read the article below: *Were we happier then?*
Note down all the points made that claim
people were happier in the past and all the
points that claim that people are happier now.

Were we happier then?

Catherine Hookham, 85, heaves a big sigh as she sits watching the evening news. Yet again crime is on the increase – a child's battered body has just been found – and hundreds of homeless teenagers roam the streets. 'Is there no end to it?' mutters Catherine as she gets up to turn off the TV. 'People were definitely much happier when I was a girl,' she says firmly. 'I'm not saying it was all sentimental like in adverts but we were certainly more contented. I know wages were much lower but your money just seemed to go further.'

But there are other reasons why Catherine feels that life has become infinitely less pleasant. Three years ago she was viciously beaten up by a mugger. As a result, she moved into an old people's home.

'This would never have happened a few years ago,' she insists. 'Then people could go out without constantly having to look over their shoulder, and mums could send their kids to play in the streets without worrying they'd be attacked or offered drugs by someone. You've only got to look at people's faces to see how depressed and worried they are.'

Alex MacGuillivary of the New Economic Foundation, an independent research centre, agrees that the quality of life in Britain has definitely deteriorated.

'Recent government figures indicate that our standard of living is rising, but they don't take into account important factors like pollution, crime and stress,' he says. 'And we're spending more and more money to combat these problems. What people want above all is security and an environment where their children can grow up to be healthy adults.'

But John McGinty of the Government's Central Statistical Office disagrees that life was better in the past. He suspects that many people look back at 'the good old days' through rose-tinted glasses.

'In 1914, when records first started, the average family were spending two-thirds of their income on food compared to 15% nowadays,' he says. 'Today we're better educated and, with shorter working hours, we have more leisure time. Housing costs about the same. So we actually have quite a bit more money to spend.'

Single mum Kerry Sparrow, 28, who works for a Bristol charity, is glad she's bringing up her 18-month-old daughter, Simi, in the nineties. She feels today's society is more open than it was in her grandmother's day. 'Single mums were ostracised years ago. They were often put into mother and baby homes and pressurised into giving up their babies for adoption,' she says. 'Some even ended up being locked away in psychiatric hospitals by people who thought mothers of illegitimate children were insane.' She insists too that her child will have much better educational opportunities than daughters born half a century earlier.

'Whether she wants to be a doctor, a bus driver or a solicitor, she can choose. I know life's not perfect in the nineties – but at least people have a bit more money and the freedom to decide how they want to live their lives.'

2 Look again at the passage and find answers to these questions.

a Catherine uses a couple of words that are in a fairly informal register. What are they? What would be the more neutral or formal equivalents of these words?

b Alex MacGuillivary uses a number of words that are in a somewhat more formal register. Name two of them. What would be slightly less formal equivalents of the words you chose?

c Find words in the text that match the following definitions. Write down the word in the phrase in which it is used.

i to speak very quietly often because you are complaining about something

ii to attack someone violently (phrasal verb)

iii someone who attacks someone else for no apparent reason

iv to fight (metaphorically)

v to treat as an outsider

vi mad

vii to surrender (phrasal verb)

Listening: For the better or for the worse?

1 ☐ Listen to two people giving their opinion on whether life has improved or not since they were children and answer these questions.

a Are their opinions closer to those of Catherine or of Kerry in the article?

b What is the main point they are each making?

2 ☐ Here – with some blanks – is the text of what the woman says on the tape. Complete as many of the blanks as you can without listening to the tape again. Then listen again and finish/check your work.

Oh, I think, I think, it's changed for the better. Really, there are, well, of course, I mean, one can (1) .... it's better and worse in different (2) .... but basically I think things are better now. I don't think there's so much (3) .... in this country, in the world. And from a sort of personal point of (4) ...., there are so many things to help you in the house, for instance. I mean, I've got a washing machine and a (5) ...., you know, and my mother didn't have any of those things. She used to (6) .... everything by hand and she had to use a brush and (7) ...., and she had to get up very early to light fires. We have central (8) .... which we can just switch on. And I think on the (9) ...., young people have a better time of it today. I mean, they have more (10) .... to travel and see the world. I think in my young (11) .... people didn't really go very much further than their own home town, you know, and people now as a (12) .... of course go abroad for their holidays or to work sometimes, so I think it's changed for the better really.

Vocabulary: Register

In the article we saw how two speakers chose to use a rather different register when they were interviewed. Alex is rather more formal than Catherine in his style of speech.

We speak in different ways with different people and we are more polite or formal with some kinds of people than with others.

Moreover, with some people – often those in the same profession as us – we have so much in common that we can use special words and the person we are talking to will know exactly what we are referring to, whereas we might have to explain our meaning more fully to someone with less shared experience.

Such aspects of language are referred to as register.

1 What could you say about the register used by the interviewer and the interviewees in the interview you listened to in Listening Exercise 1 (the tapescript is on page 170)? What factors make them use this kind of register as opposed to something rather different?

2 The sorts of things that affect the register people use when speaking to one another in English are:

- age;
- sex;
- the length of acquaintanceship;
- the closeness of the relationship;
- work or social status;
- the nature of the specific situation;
- who else is present.

How might these factors affect the way people speak to each other in your language?

3 Arrange these situations on a scale from very formal register to very informal register.

a two long-standing working colleagues (male, in their 30s) discussing a joint work project

b a father and 17-year-old daughter discussing her (poor) exam results

c a middle-aged boss interviewing a school-leaver for a job

d two teenage friends discussing their plans for the weekend

e a teenage girl asking a peer to lend her her favourite jeans

f a mayor congratulating a local business person publicly on a successful export drive

g a brother and sister arguing about whose turn it is to do a household chore

h a husband and wife reminiscing on their 25th wedding anniversary

i a boy and girl, both aged 19, out on their first date together

j a junior secretary telling her female boss about a problem she is having at work

k an elderly aunt discussing the habits of the young with her young niece

l two students on their first day at college meeting for the first time

4 Look at the different groups of people in the pictures. Consider the following questions about the picture or pictures which your teacher asks you to focus on.

a Would the register used in a conversation between the people in this picture probably be formal, neutral or informal?

b Would the people in this picture share any words or expressions that might be unclear to other groups of people?

c What characteristics of the people in the pictures helped you answer questions a and b?

5 Read these two dialogues. Which of the pictures do you think they relate to?

A: Good morning. I hope you slept well?
B: Yes, thank you. I was very comfortable.
A: Have you already decided what you would like to do first today?
B: Yes, I was wondering if I could possibly start by meeting someone from the sales and marketing department?

A: Hi! How's things?
B: Awful! I didn't sleep a wink last night, I was so worried about the test. What about you?
A: Oh, I'm OK. Shall we grab a coffee?
B: No, I've got to meet Jim in two minutes. I'll catch you later.

6 🖭 Listen to two dialogues. Which of the pictures do they relate to?

7 Work with a partner and follow these instructions.

1 Write a dialogue between the people in two of the pictures. Both your dialogues should be on the same subject – your teacher will tell you which pictures to write for and what the subject of your dialogues should be. Your two dialogues should illustrate the difference in register appropriate to the situations in the two pictures you are writing for.

2 Take it in turns to read your dialogues to the other students in the class. Can they guess which pictures the dialogues are based on?

8 Here are some words which would have different first associations if used by different groups of people. Explain what the difference in meaning would be for each group.

a register – linguists, teachers, musicians
b theatre – actors, doctors
c to retreat – soldiers, religious people, medical researchers studying epidemics, psychologists
d silk – lawyers, dressmakers
e to cover – teachers, insurance sales staff, soldiers, journalists
f concentration – psychologists, chemists, geographers
g a cue – actors, snooker-players
h turnover – accountants, bankers, sociologists
i a drill – dentists, soldiers, road-builders, language teachers
j reserve – sportspeople, cooks, restaurant owners, psychologists, auctioneers
k a report – teachers, journalists, soldiers, nurses, business people
l a bug – computer programmers, doctors, zoologists, spies

9 Name at least three professions that might have different associations for each of these words. Use a dictionary to help you if necessary.

crown   nail   proof   stock   net

Speaking: How life changes

1 Discuss the questions below with a partner. You should discuss the questions, however, three times, each time as if you were in the different roles specified below.

a In what ways, in your opinion, has life changed?
b How do you think life will be different for the next generation?

1 Discuss the questions first as if you were a couple of old people (friends since their childhood) convinced that life is getting worse all the time.
2 Now discuss the questions as if one of you was a young person convinced that things are getting better. The other person is the young person's much older boss, someone who feels that most, if not all, things are worse than they used to be in his or her youth.
3 Finally, discuss the questions as if you were two strangers of much the same age meeting on a train. Neither of you has a particularly strong opinion about the subject but you are keen to keep the subject going to help the long journey pass more quickly.

2 As a class discuss how the different roles you took on in the previous exercise affected your conversations.

Grammar: Modals

Modal verbs have a number of things in common.
- Modal verbs are all used with main verbs to add something about the speaker's attitude to the meaning of the main verb.
- They are all the same in all persons (i.e. they have no third person singular *s*).
- None of them use *do* to form their questions or negatives.
- They are followed by the infinitive without *to* of other verbs (except for *ought*).

1 Look again at the article at the beginning of this unit. Underline all the examples of modals you can find in it. What is the meaning which the modal adds in each case?

2 Some of the verbs which are referred to in English grammar as modals, their forms and their usages are shown in this chart. (The others are in a similar chart in the next unit.) Below are some example sentences to add to the chart. Write the letter of the example beside the appropriate category in the 'Meanings' column of the chart.

Can
a How many people can be seated in this hall?
b Can I help you?
c I can ski quite well.
d She can be very nice if she's in a good mood.
e Of course you can have some juice if you'd like some.
f You can wash up and then you can do the beds.
g Can you thread this needle for me, please?
h It can't be true. I know he'd never do a thing like that.

Could
i It couldn't be John – he's in London today.
j Could I use your phone?
k Could I carry your suitcase for you?
l Anne could talk when she was 18 months old.
m Could you help me move the piano?
n It could rain later on (but I don't think it will).
o I could buy a new car if I got the job.

May
p I may go to the concert if I finish my work in time.
q May I have a chocolate? Yes, of course you may.

Might
r I might go to the concert if I can only get my work finished.
s Might I accompany you to the ball?

Must
t That must be his sister – she looks just like him.
u We really must go now.

Shall
v We shall overcome all oppression some day.
w Shall I open the door for you?
x How shall I get to your house?
y Shall we go to the theatre this evening?

Modal verb	Notes on usage	Meanings
can	Infinitive form if needed = *to be able to*	Ability ...... Negative certainty ...... Theoretical possibility ...... Habitual possibility ...... Giving permission ...... Offering ...... Requesting ...... Ordering ......
could	Not used for specific ability in past (i.e. when meaning = *managed to*) – must then use *was/were able to*	General ability in the past ...... Negative certainty ...... Conditional (= *would be able to*) ...... Weak possibility ...... Asking for permission (not giving it) ...... Offering ...... Requesting ......
may		Possibility ...... Asking for and giving permission (rather formal) ......
might		Asking for permission (not giving it) ...... Possibility (less possible than *may*) ......
must	Infinitive form if needed = *to have to*	Obligation ...... Deduction ......
shall	Now used only with *I* and *we*	Simple future ...... Offering ...... Suggesting ...... Requesting instructions or advice ......

3 🔊 Listen to the tape. Explain what the difference in meaning is between the pairs of sentences which you hear.

4 Write examples of your own for each of the usages of modals listed in the chart in Exercise 2.

Writing: A report

1 If you need to use English for work or study purposes, you may well need to be able to write a report. Like magazine articles, a report may be primarily interested in conveying information.

However, there are some basic differences between the style of reports and articles. What are these differences?

What are the main characteristics of a report?

2 Here is an example of a short report. The headings have got mixed up. Read it and put the headings back in the right place. Now give the report a title.

CONCLUSION

Recently we carried out a survey into how people feel about new technology and its influence on people's domestic lives. We gave 156 people a questionnaire and received replies from all but six of them. Twenty-five of our respondents are teenagers, ninety are in their twenties and the remainder are thirty years old or above. The six people who did not return their questionnaires are all in the thirty-plus age group.

EFFECTS OF TECHNOLOGY

We asked people how many of the following examples of modern technology they possessed at home – a computer, a fax machine, an answerphone, a modem with Internet connection, a video camera, a microwave, a jacuzzi. We also asked them to add any other examples of modern technology which they had recently acquired. We then requested them to indicate how much they used each of the items of modern technology that they reported possessing. Finally, we asked people to assess the extent to which these items of modern technology had had a positive or a negative effect on their lives. At this point in the questionnaire we asked our respondents not only to tick boxes, but also to add comments explaining how exactly an item of technology had affected their lives in either positive or negative ways.

INTRODUCTION

All of our respondents had at least three of the items on our list with a microwave, a computer and a video camera being the items most frequently possessed. Only one of our respondents possessed a jacuzzi. Twenty-three of the respondents had all of the other items but the jacuzzi. Half of the respondents added at least one other example of modern technology recently acquired for the home: these included automatic garage doors, burglar alarm, sandwich toaster, cordless iron, CD player. The younger the respondent, the more likely they were to use all the items they had except the microwave. This was most popular with the over-thirties. Of all the items of new technology we had listed, the video camera was least frequently used – only once a month by the teenagers and four times a year by older age groups.

USE OF TECHNOLOGY

When we asked people whether they felt that new technology was affecting their lives in a positive or a negative way, all of the teenagers and 72% of the people in the middle age group said that they felt that the effects of new technology were basically positive. Sixty-five per cent of the older age group, on the other hand, felt that new technology had more negative than positive effects on their lives. The most frequent advantages of new technology listed in the verbal responses were (in order of frequency of mention):

1 saving time;
2 making communications easier;
3 educational;
4 fun.

The negative effects mentioned were:

1 technology makes people lazy;
2 machines become more important than people;
3 the machines are always going wrong.

QUESTIONNAIRE USED

In conclusion, new technology is having a significant effect on domestic life. For most people, especially the young, these effects are positive. Older people, although they use technology only marginally less than young people do, find it harder to adapt to it and are more likely to see the problems in our dependence on it than are teenagers.

3 You are now going to conduct a survey of your class's attitudes and will then write a report of your findings. Follow these instructions.

1 Divide into four groups of equal size. Each group is going to take one of the following topics and will conduct a survey on it and then write a report relating to it.
   • The problems facing the young today
   • The magazine reading habits of the class
   • The good and bad points of living in this town
   • Attitudes towards smoking.

2 Prepare a list of five to ten questions to ask about the topic you chose. The majority of your questions should encourage precise answers so that you can give statistical feedback after your survey. You may well want to include some more open questions but make sure that most of your questions are reasonably closed.

3 You must interview all the students in the class, including the members of your own group. Decide how you are going to organise your interviews – you could, for example, each take responsibility either for a group of students (so that you ask all the questions to a limited number of students) or for a group of questions (so that you ask the same one or two questions to all the students in the class).

4 Carry out your interviews, taking careful notes of the answers you receive.

5 Share your findings with the other students in your group.

4 You are now going to plan your report. Read the following advice on planning the beginning and end of a report.

Remember that the main characteristics of a good report are that it should be informative and clear.

The achievement of these aims is often helped by dividing the report into sections and giving each section a clear heading. The first heading will often be *Introduction* and the last heading will often be *Conclusion.*
It is important to begin and end your report in an effective way.

Introductions and conclusions need to be:
– appropriate in content;
– well presented;
– clear;
– accurate.

These characteristics are required throughout by a report but they are particularly significant at the beginning and end as a reader may well pay particular attention to these sections.

5 ⌷ Listen to the following ways of introducing and concluding a report on *The Magazine Reading Habits of the Class.* Do you consider that they make good or bad introductory or concluding remarks for a report? If there is a problem, is it connected with content, presentation, clarity or accuracy?

6 Read the following advice on structuring the body of a report.

Clarity is also often helped by numbering the points being made. For example,
   Problems with employment
   Young people today face a number of problems related to employment.
1 Young people are increasingly likely to face the problem of unemployment at some point in their careers. This is particularly true for young people with few qualifications, but it also affects those with higher education looking for work in their specialism.
2 Employers tend to pay young people less even though they may be doing the same work as their elders. This problem was noted by approximately one half of those interviewed.
3 Young people enter work with high expectations of bettering the world and/or advancing themselves. These expectations are often disappointed by reality.

7 Discuss in your group how best to organise your report. Think about these questions.

a What information should be contained in the introduction?
b What other section headings should you use?
c Could numbering help the presentation of your report? If so, how?
d What should go in the conclusion?

8 Each member of the group should now draft a report individually, referring to other students wherever necessary for information about their findings and for advice on how to present the material.

9 Exchange your drafts with another student who has written up the same survey. Look at your partner's report critically. Think about:

• content
• presentation
• clarity
• accuracy

Suggest improvements to each other's work and rewrite your reports in the light of the suggestions made.

10 Work in groups of four. Each group should have one student who worked on each of the topics. Read each other's reports. Question each other on any points that were not clear in the reports.

Game, set and match
Sports reports

The main aspects of language worked on in this unit are:

- listening to sports reports
- writing accurately – grammar and vocabulary
- more modals
- idioms
- assessing your progress

Warm-up: Sports

1 In two minutes how many English names for sports can the class brainstorm?

2 Which of the sports listed have you tried? Did you enjoy them?

Would you like to try the others one day? Why (not)?

Listening: Sports reports

1 Listen to some extracts from sports news reports. Which sport is being talked about? Write the number of the report against the appropriate picture.

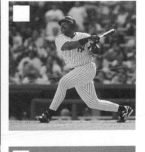

2 Listen again and for each sport write two or three words or expressions from the commentary which helped you decide which sport was being commented on.

There are not commentaries for all the sports illustrated. Write down some words which are particularly associated with the extra sports.

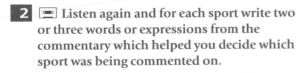

3 You are going to listen to a complete sports report from a reporter who was able to accompany a top motor racing driver. Before listening, decide how you think the reporter felt as they raced around the track. What sort of language do you think he might have used to express his feelings?

4 ▭ Now listen to the tape. Did you predict correctly any of the language he used?

Did you feel the reporter conveyed his feelings well? Why, or why not?

Would you like to have a similar sort of experience? Why, or why not?

Reading: Warming-up for table tennis

About five minutes before you are due on the table seek out a quiet spot where you can privately run through a brief warm-up routine. Keep your tracksuit top or sweatshirt on throughout.

Start jogging gently on the spot for about a minute, keeping the rest of your limbs relaxed. Follow this with ten or so standing squats or perhaps thirty seconds of bouncing on the spot. These two exercises will make your heart pump a little faster because they involve the use of large muscle groups in the legs.

Now move on to a series of stretching and loosening exercises, concentrating in particular on those muscle groups and joints which get most use during a match. Here is a list of those exercises most favoured by the England squad.

– Neck rolling.

– Straight arm circles from the shoulder, clockwise and anti-clockwise.

– Shoulder shrugs with arms by the sides.

– Upper body rotation from the waist with forearms held at shoulder height.

– Hip circling with hands at the waist (imagine you're using a hula hoop).

– Knee circling with the knees slightly bent and the legs held together. Rest your hands just above each knee to aid balance.

– Roll your ankle joints by pivoting on your toe, one leg at a time.

– Forearm circling from the elbow, clockwise and anti-clockwise.

– Wrist rolling by clapping both hands together 'prayer' fashion.

This brief warm-up routine – and later the pre-match knock-up – will provide you with the opportunity to address the game in hand. Think about your opponent, his strengths and weaknesses. Can he handle spin? Is he quick about the table? How well does he react to changes in pace? If questions like these are running through your mind, then congratulations – you're thinking tactics.

1 The expression *warm-up*, which is often used by language teachers, comes originally from sport and refers to a group of exercises done to get a sportsman or woman ready for action. Discuss these questions with a partner.

a Would it be necessary to do some kind of warm-up before playing each of the sports pictured in Listening Exercise 1? Why, or why not?
b How might the kind of warm-up done differ from sport to sport? Why would there be such differences?

2 Read the text. The best way to check that you have understood the text is to do the exercises suggested in it.

3 Without using words, demonstrate what these words from the text mean.

> jogging   relaxed   squat   anti-clockwise   shrug   wrist
> waist   clapping

4 Answer the following questions.

a What is the difference between *warm-up* and *knock-up*?
b What does the word *tactics* suggest at the end of the text?
c Why do the questions quoted by the writer of the text suggest that a person is thinking tactics?
d How might a player's game be affected by the answers he or she gives to the tactical questions about their opponent's play posed in the last paragraph?

5 If you play a sport of some kind, do you do a similar kind of warm-up? Or would some other exercises be more useful? If you are familiar with other warm-up exercises, describe them to other students in the class in such a precise way that the other students can try them out.

Vocabulary: Choosing the right word

Choosing the right vocabulary item is also an important aspect of using English accurately. When writing, even more perhaps than when speaking, you have to choose the right word for the context. This can be a problem in English when there are frequently several words for one concept but only one of these is right in any particular context. A referee has much the same role as an umpire, for example, but football or rugby always use referees whereas tennis and cricket require umpires.

1 The text on warming up for table tennis used a large number of precise words to explain the exercises. Look at the passage again and answer these questions.

a What words did it use to describe precise parts of the body?
b What words did it use to describe precise movements?

Your teacher will give you either the name of a part of the body or a phrase describing an action. Point to the part of the body or perform the action. The rest of the class should guess which word your teacher gave you.

2 Here are some more questions focusing on the right words for use when talking about sports.

a What is the difference between a racket and a bat? Which of these sports uses a racket and which a bat?

- tennis
- table tennis
- squash
- cricket
- baseball

b The words on the left refer to places where the different sports on the right are played. Which place is associated with each of the sports?

court	running
rink	football
pitch	golf
course	motor racing
track	ice hockey
	roller-skating
	rugby
	tennis
	horse racing
	ice skating
	netball
	cricket

c Match the words and expressions associated with scoring in the left-hand column with their sports in the right-hand column.

love	archery
nil	ice skating
five point nine	cricket
a bull's eye	football
a century	tennis

Explain what each expression means.

Grammar: More modals

You will meet a tall, dark, handsome man

1 Look again at the table tennis text and underline the examples of modal verbs you can find in the text.

Identify the uses of the modals you underlined from the chart in the previous unit (page 77) and the one below.

2 As in the previous unit you have some example sentences to match to the chart. Write the letter of the example from the list beside the appropriate category in the chart.

Should

a He recommended that we should make an early start on our journey.
b You should always do what your mother says.
c The train should be here soon. It's already five minutes late.
d I'm sorry that you should feel that way.
e If I won the lottery, I should buy a new house.
f If he should turn up, tell him I've gone home.

Will

g You will meet a tall, dark, handsome man in the next few days.
h The car just won't start.
i He *will* keep smoking even though he knows I detest the habit.
j She will always bring us flowers from her garden whenever she comes round.
k If you will wash the dishes, I'll dry them.
l Will you come to the party with me?
m It'll be fine tomorrow, according to the forecast.

Would

n It was in Paris that he had the idea that would make him a fortune.
o Would you close the window, please?
p If she would stop biting her nails, she could be a model.
q We would spend all our holidays at the beach.
r I would stay here for ever if I didn't have to go back to work.

Ought

s They ought to call us next. We got here before everyone else in the waiting room.
t You ought to go to that new hairdresser's.

3 📼 Listen to the tape and explain what the difference in meaning is between the pairs of sentences which you hear.

Modal verb	Notes on usage	Meaning
should		Expressing conditional (1st person) .... After *if* or *in case* (with any person) to indicate less strong possibility .... Advising .... Strong probability (it's logical) .... After various adjectives which stress personal reaction or attitude ...... After a number of verbs, e.g. *suggest*, *insist*, to stress that something is important ....
will	Used with 2nd and 3rd persons and also, increasingly, with *I* and *we*	Simple future .... Predicting .... Willingness .... Polite invitations and requests .... Refusals .... Habits, characteristic behaviour .... Criticising (when *will* is stressed) ....
would		Conditional .... Talking about the future in the past .... Past habits, characteristic behaviour .... Polite requests .... Willingness (after *I wish*, *if*) ....
ought to	The only modal used with *to*	Advising .... Strong probability (it's logical) ....

4 Write sentences about a sport you know using the following modals.

- will
- would
- should
- ought
- must
- can
- may
- might

5 Look back at some of the texts you have worked with in this book so far – either at tape transcripts or at written texts. What examples of modals can you find? Which uses of modals do they illustrate?

6 If you have access to other texts in English – perhaps to an issue of a newspaper or magazine or to a novel or short story – see if you can find any other examples of modals in use.

If possible write down ten sentences using modals in different ways. Which uses of modals do your sentences illustrate?

7 Compare the examples which you found with those found by other students. Which of the uses of modals (from the charts on pages 77 and 84) have you found examples for?

Invent some additional examples of your own for any of the uses that you do not have an example for.

Vocabulary: Idioms

Idioms have their origins in various areas of life and sometimes a knowledge of the origin can help you to understand – and remember – the meaning of the idiom. For example, *to be blinkered* means *to have a very narrow view*. The idiom originates in horse riding where blinkers are leather squares fixed to the sides of a horse's eyes to prevent it from seeing sideways.

1 A number of English idioms have their origins in sports. Here are some idioms originating in different sports – riding, sailing, football, boxing, cricket, chess and archery.

Match the idiom on the left with its definition on the right.

a to be out for the count
b to have had a good innings
c to spur someone on to something
d to give someone free rein
e to be at the helm
f to rock the boat
g to be champing at the bit
h to do something off one's own bat
i to be on the ball
j to reach stalemate
k to take the wind out of someone's sails
l to have more than one string to one's bow

1 to be impatient to get started
2 to be exhausted, deeply asleep
3 to disturb someone's self-confidence
4 to act on one's own initiative
5 to be quick and alert
6 to be in charge
7 to allow someone to do what they want
8 to have an alternative open to one
9 to encourage someone
10 to disturb a pleasant situation
11 to get to a stage in a dispute where no action can be taken by either side
12 to have had a long, successful life/term of office

2 Identify which sport each of the idioms has its origins in. Match the pictures to the literal meaning of the idiom.

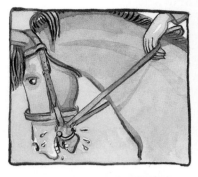

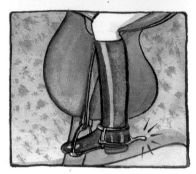

3 Explain how the original meaning of the remaining six idioms led to their metaphoric meanings.

4 Choose one of the idioms from Exercise 1 to complete the sentences below. You may need to make slight changes to make the idioms fit grammatically in some cases.

a Unfortunately the peace talks have, once again, ...

b With Jack ...., I think the project should succeed. He's had a lot of experience of managing similar projects.

c Go to university and take a teacher training course. Then, if you can't make a career on the stage, it won't be a disaster. You'll ....

d Look at those children. They're really .... I suppose they are exhausted from all that running around on the beach all day.

e I'm very impressed by the way Jill has tidied up her room. And I didn't even suggest she should do it. She did it entirely ....

f Let her approach the project in her own way. In my experience, it's usually better .... They sometimes then develop a very useful new approach.

g I think we'd better get moving as soon as we can. The kids are already .... And if we don't get started soon, they'll start getting fractious.

h Everything was going smoothly at work until the new deputy manager came along and .... Most of us are on the lookout for new jobs to apply for at the moment.

i Sheila deserves to get the job. She's really ...., unlike some of the other applicants.

j I would never have had the confidence to apply for the job if you hadn't ....

k He was addressing the staff quite happily when she .... by asking him a question that absolutely floored him.

l She had been chairperson of the committee for 25 years when she retired last month. She'd certainly .... The last two chairpeople before her had only lasted for a couple of months, I believe.

Writing: Being accurate

Writing accurately is partly a matter of choosing the right words. We did some work on the question of precision in vocabulary choice earlier in this unit. Writing accurately is, however, also a matter both of avoiding grammar mistakes and of presenting your writing in a clear and unambiguous way. This section gives you practice in all these aspects of accuracy.

1 Here are fourteen of the most frequent errors which foreign learners of English make with English grammar.

- confusing the present perfect and the past simple
- using the present simple or continuous instead of the present perfect in *for* or *since* clauses
- confusing the present simple and the present continuous
- using the wrong pattern of tenses in a conditional sentence
- using the wrong tense in a future adverbial clause of time
- confusing the gerund and the infinitive
- using the wrong preposition
- using the wrong word order with adverbials
- using the wrong word order in reported or indirect questions
- incorrect agreement of subject and verb
- treating uncountable nouns like countable nouns
- using *the* with plural or uncountable nouns when making general statements
- confusing *too* and *very*
- not using articles correctly

Here are a number of sentences containing characteristic mistakes.

First, identify which of the errors listed above is illustrated in each sentence. Then correct the sentences.

a Jane likes very much tennis although her brother doesn't like it at all.
b We'll be in touch as soon as we'll know when we will be playing.
c If you would have been there, you hadn't believed your eyes.
d They are really looking forward to take part in the Olympics next year.
e Everybody know that Brazilian people plays very good football.
f As soon as the athletes had arrived in New York, their manager has contacted his American office.
g The result of the match will depend of many factors.
h The team plays much better this season than it did last year.
i If the weather will become a little cooler, they will have a real chance of beating the other team.
j We have as yet too few informations about what equipments there are in the gym.
k She's been practising too hard for the competition   she's sure to win.
l The life is hard for an athlete in his or her thirties.
m I wonder when will we learn the results of the game.
n When the whistle goes you have to stop to play.
o Our Russian team won match.
p We are playing squash every Saturday – why don't you come with us next week?
q We are top of the league since 1994.
r United States does better than United Kingdom at many sports.

2 You are going to concentrate on accuracy while writing an essay about any sport you have experience of and covering at least some of the following aspects. (If you are not interested in sport, you may choose to write about any indoor game that you enjoy, e.g. chess, cards, dominoes.)

- why I like this sport (or why I don't like it)
- what you need to play it – equipment
- where to do or watch it
- basic aims and rules of the game
- how it is scored
- advice to novices
- one or more memorable experiences I've had playing or watching this sport

Choose the sport you are going to write about. Make a list of all the vocabulary you can think of which is associated with talking about your sport. Use a dictionary if necessary. You may also find it useful, if it is possible, to look at a sports report in an English language newspaper relating to your specific sport and to note down any further useful words or expressions that you find there.

3 Form groups of three or four. Ask and tell each other about your sports. Try to talk about each of the seven aspects listed above in Exercise 2. Use as much of the specialist vocabulary you collected in the previous exercise as possible.

4 Follow these instructions to write your essay.

1 Prepare a plan for your essay.
2 Write the essay.
3 Exchange essays with one of the students you worked with in Exercise 3.
4 Read the other student's essay. Has the student written accurate English, do you think? Mark any points where you feel there may be a language error. Also think about how the content of the essay could be improved. For example, is anything unclear? Would you like any further information about something that is mentioned in the essay?
5 Write at least three comments or questions about the essay for the other student, asking for further information or clarification.
6 Rewrite your essay, taking into account the comments and questions made by the other student.
7 Give the re-drafted essay to your teacher for marking.

Study skills: Assessing your progress

At your level of English, it can often be hard to see how you are making progress. After all, you can do most of the things you need to do in English without too much difficulty and there is not much grammar left to 'do'.

Most students at your level need, above all, to improve their accuracy, to expand their vocabulary and to extend their speaking and listening skills. However, it can be hard to make yourself aware of just how much progress you are making in these areas; it was much easier to feel your progress when your English was at a lower level.

One of the best ways you can assess your progress is by looking back at how your English was when you began this coursebook and how it is now. Try at least some of these activities. They should give you some sense of the progress you are making. In addition to that, they will also help you to learn even more in that they are in themselves revision activities.

1 Look back at a piece of writing that you did earlier in the course. Do another piece of writing on the same subject, trying to include some of the language that you have learnt over the last few weeks. Ask your teacher to compare the two pieces of work.

2 Think about what you were doing in the week when you began this coursebook. Can you think of any situations at that time where you had difficulty with either speaking or understanding spoken English? Do you think that you would find those situations equally difficult now?

3 Look back at notes you have made of vocabulary and other aspects of grammar over the last few weeks. How much do you remember of what you have written down?

4 If possible, listen to a recording made of yourself speaking English at the beginning of this course. Do you feel that you could express yourself more accurately and more fluently now? If possible, make a recording of yourself speaking English now, so that you can listen to it again when you finish this coursebook to see how much more progress you have made.

5 Look back at the texts you studied earlier in this book. Do you think you can understand them more easily now than you did the first time round?

6 Test a partner. Ask him or her some questions about things that you have learnt in your English classes together. How well did you both do?

7 Look at some of the exercises which you found particularly difficult when you first tried them. Do they seem more straightforward when you try them second time around?

Shoot with care
Instructions

The main
aspects of
language
worked on in
this unit are:

- following and giving instructions
- intonation
- structures with particular verbs
- spelling
- English and your own language

Warm-up: Giving instructions

1 ⊟ Listen to some people giving instructions about paper-folding and try to do what they say.

Was it easy to follow their instructions? Why (not)?

2 Discuss with the rest of the class:

a Have you any experience of particularly bad or particularly good instructions?
b What makes a set of instructions either good or bad?

3 Work in pairs and follow these instructions.

1 Take a pencil and two pieces of paper each. Sit back to back.
2 On one of your pieces of paper, draw a diagram or picture in any way that you like.
3 Take it in turns to describe your diagram or picture to the other person. Your partner must use his or her other piece of paper in order to draw what you describe – without looking at your original drawing. If possible record your instructions.
4 Compare the second drawing with the original. Discuss how the original could have been more clearly described for the person trying to do the second drawing.

Reading: Instructions

1 Read this extract from *Learn to Video in a Weekend*, a manual on making effective videos. Make notes of the basic points which this extract is trying to put across.

2 Note down all the words and expressions in the video instructions which have a specific technical meaning connected with video recording, e.g. *shot length*, *editing*.

A SENSE OF TIME

Getting a sense of appropriate shot lengths by developing your sense of screen time and the skill of editing

SHOT LENGTHS

Video-making necessitates that you develop a sense of screen time and the skills to manipulate it. Each time you press the "record" button, think about the length of the shot. With static shots of stationary subjects, shot length is determined by the amount of information the audience needs to take in. In general, the wider the shot and the more detail it shows, the longer it needs to be on screen. As a guide, allow a minimum of three seconds from the start of recording.

ACTION SUBJECTS

Any static shots involving continuous action, activity, or slow movement – a view of a market scene – will need to be up to half as long again. Where you are following action with camera movements, it is important to let the camcorder settle momentarily at the end of the shot before cutting. For shots that involve words which the audience must read, allow about three words per second, then add one third of the total for slow readers.

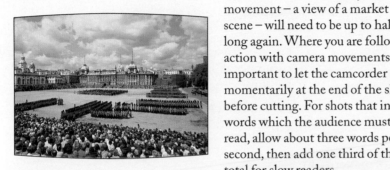

CUTTING POINTS

Much of the time, cutting points and shot lengths will be determined by the action you are recording and the degree to which the subject will hold the interest of your audience. With static or panning shots of action subjects, such as a skier traversing downhill, the logic is simple – cut once the subject has left the frame. It is often essential when shooting activity subjects that the viewers see the action from start to end. They will feel cheated if you cut too soon.

SOUND & PROGRAMME LENGTH

Timing has to do with the length of individual shots and the overall length of the programme you make. Often, shot length is determined by the sound you are recording, so keep listening. The Best Man's speech at a wedding or a guide's description of a place of interest could be spoiled if the audience does not hear the essential parts. Programme lengths will vary according to the subject matter, but you should always keep your audience in mind when deciding how much to shoot. Weddings and sports events may take a fixed time, but do not necessarily demand that they subsequently be seen in their entirety. If the audience get bored, you will lose their attention, so it is always better to be brief.

3 Discuss the following with a partner.

a Have you ever used a video camera? If so, which of these techniques were you already aware of and which were new to you?

b If you have never used a video camera, do you think these instructions are appropriate for a beginner (as they are intended to be)?

4 In what ways does the writer try to put his ideas across effectively? List as many points as you can and then compare your ideas with those of other students.

Writing: Instructions

Write a set of instructions of your own using all the devices discussed in Reading Exercise 4. Choose any one of the following subjects:

Making a sound-track for your video;
Taking photographs;

A beginner's guide to learning English;
Using body language.

Speaking: Intonation

1 🖭 Listen to each of these dialogues spoken twice. In each case, how does Jane sound – interested or bored?

a BILL: If you click on this icon, then the paragraph you've selected is immediately boxed.
JANE: Really.

b BILL: Fast forward until I say when.
JANE: OK.

c BILL: I made a fantastic cold soup using sour cream, soda water, cucumber, dill and boiled eggs last night.
JANE: Did you?

d BILL: Do you know how this kite works?
JANE: No, but Kathy'd know.

2 An inappropriate intonation pattern can sound strange and, often, amusing. Practise reading the following in the styles suggested.

a It's easy to spell-check any document by just clicking here with your mouse. The program will then search for any words which are not in its dictionary and, when it finds one, it will ask you if you want to change the spelling or not. The computer will suggest how it thinks the word should be spelt.
Read in the style of a politician giving a campaign speech prior to an important election.

b Catherine Parker and John Taylor have announced their engagement. Their wedding will take place on Thursday, 30th August at the Church of the Holy Trinity in Bridge Street and the reception will take place at Catherine's parents' house.
Read as if by the jilted boy- or girlfriend of one of the engaged couple.

c It's been raining all day in the north and east of the country but elsewhere has seen a pleasant day with considerable sunshine for the time of year. The rain is likely to move away overnight allowing most of the country to enjoy a dry and relatively warm day tomorrow. Temperatures may reach 20 degrees Centigrade in the south.
Read in the style of a sports commentator.

3 **When describing intonation patterns in English we use the terms *fall*, *rise* and *fall-rise*. These terms refer to the way the voice goes up and down in the course of a particular utterance. If someone uses a *fall* pattern, then their voice goes down so that at the end of the phrase or sentence it is lower than it was at the beginning. In a *rise* pattern, the speaker's voice is higher at the end of the phrase or sentence than it was at the beginning. In a *fall-rise* pattern, the speaker's voice first goes down and then goes up again.**

 Listen to the tape and repeat the examples of each of the patterns.

Which of the three intonation patterns – fall, rise or fall-rise – is the speaker using in each case?

Explain how the different intonation patterns used affect the meaning in each case.

4 **Practise fall and rise intonation patterns by saying the utterances below in the two different ways indicated.**

a You press this button, don't you?
  i You're sure, no answer is needed.
  ii You're unsure and want an answer.
b What's this knob for?
  i It's the first time you've asked this question.
  ii It's the second time you've asked this question.
c They won a prize with the video they took of their holiday.
  i You are sure that they did.
  ii You're not sure whether they really did.
d Their photos were good.
  i There's no doubt about it.
  ii You haven't seen the photos and want to know.

5 Answering questions with just one word can sound abrupt. Adding a little bit more not only helps to keep the conversation going, but it also allows you to use a fall-rise pattern, so indicating with your voice a desire to continue talking.

Do the following exercise to practise answering questions.

1 First write one-word answers to each of these questions.
  a What's your name?
  b Where do you come from?
  c How old are you?
  d Have you any brothers or sisters?
  e Do you like learning English?
  f It's a lovely day, isn't it?
  g Have you ever used a video camera?
  h What was the weather like at the weekend?
  i Who's your favourite singer?
  j Shall we go to London on Saturday?

2 Now add an extra phrase to each of your one-word answers.
  e.g. What's your name?
  William, but most people call me Bill.
3 Work with a partner. Ask and answer the questions, using the fuller answers that you prepared and a fall-rise intonation.

Grammar: Patterns associated with particular verbs

1 Look at these four common verb patterns in English.

a verb + infinitive — They wanted to make a film.

b verb + object + infinitive — They told us to shoot a lot of film.

c verb + gerund — The producer recommended shooting in the early morning.

d verb + object + preposition + gerund/noun — The weather prevented us from shooting the scene.

Put each of the verbs below into the appropriate group (a, b, c or d). Notice that some may fit into more than one category. Use a dictionary to help you, if necessary.

> accuse admit advise afford allow arrange attempt avoid compel consent deprive encourage fail forbid happen imagine instruct manage miss permit remind subject suggest

2 Divide groups a, b, c and d into sub-groups depending on their meaning.

3 Write sentences – about making videos, if you wish, or about any other topic of your choice – for each of the four columns. Try to write one sentence which will make sense with all the words in the group in it. For example, for group a, you could write:

The producer | happened / consented / managed / failed / wanted / arranged / attempted | to make the film in three months.

Note that a different sentence is needed for *afford*, as *afford* almost always follows *can(not)* or *could(n't)*, e.g. *They couldn't afford to shoot the film on location.*

a verb + infinitive	*b* verb + object + infinitive	*c* verb + gerund	*d* verb + object + preposition + gerund/noun
want	tell	recommend	prevent somebody from doing something

Vocabulary: Spelling

1 Look back at the text on making a video. Are there any words in the text which you feel could be a problem from the point of view of spelling? If so, why?

2 Although English spelling may seem totally illogical, it does have some rules which learners can make use of. Write down the rules which each of these sets of words illustrates.

a hopeful, beautiful, grateful, hopefully, beautifully, gratefully
Example: Adjectives ending in *-ful* have only one *l*. The *l* doubles to make the adverb.
b achieve, believe, receive, ceiling, priest, brief, thief, siege, deceit, perceive
c occurring, motored, opening, suffering, preferred, preferable, upsetting, referred, deterred, entering, beginning, visiting
d travelled, equalled, rebelled, compelled, quarrelled, distilled
e hurry, rely, try, happy, marry, baby, study, hurried, reliable, tried, happier, married, babies, studies
f trying, marrying, studying, babyish

3 Below are twenty words which many people find particularly difficult to spell. Check that you understand the meaning of each of the words. Then follow the instructions.

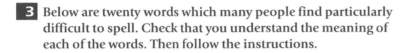

accommodation address beautiful committee February foreign government inoculate instalment necessary parallel parliament privilege professor pronunciation psychiatrist recommend separate skilful supersede

1 Write a paragraph using as many of the words as possible.
2 Look at the words again and learn the spelling of those you find particularly difficult – perhaps you can think of a mnemonic to help you. For example, two *rs* for two red cheeks in embarrass.
3 Take it in turns to test a partner on the spelling of these words.

4 Can you think of any words which are similar in your language and in English but which are spelt differently in English? The word *address* in English has two *ds*, for example, whereas in many other languages a similar word has only one *d*.

Study skills: English and your own language

English is originally an Anglo-Saxon language with many words similar to those in German, Dutch or the Scandinavian languages. However, invasion by the French in the eleventh century led to a large influx of words from French. Scholars drew on Latin and Greek to form many of the more literary words in the language. Over the centuries different nationalities have been particularly influential in particular spheres and this is reflected in English vocabulary: Italian has had a particular influence on music and the plastic arts, French on ballet, diplomacy and cooking, German on philosophy, for example. The British have long been travellers and drew on the languages of the countries they visited or colonised to enrich their own language still further, so that even languages which are linguistically very distant from English have had some influence on English – *mohair*, *sherbet*, *harem* and *assassin* are some of the words that have come into English from Arabic; *karate* and *typhoon* from Japan; *barbecue*, *canoe* and *potato* from the West Indies and so on.

1 Brainstorm as many examples as you can of words or expressions that your first language has given to English. For each of the words you think of, note (a) the meaning and (b) the pronunciation. These may not always be the same as in the original language.

2 Note down any words you can think of which are false friends in English for people who speak your language. False friends are words which look more or less the same but do not, in fact, have the same meaning. For example *brat* in English means a spoilt child, whereas in Russian it means simply *brother*!

Borrowing words and expressions is usually a two-way process. As English is used so widely in international business and the media today, it is probable that your own language has taken in some words and expressions from the English language.

3 Brainstorm as many examples as you can of English words or expressions that are used in your first language.

4 Look at some newspapers or magazines in your own language to see if you can find any more such words or expressions.

5 For each of the words you think of, note (a) the original English meaning and (b) the original English pronunciation. These may not always be precisely the same as the meaning and the pronunciation used by speakers of your language.

The main aspects of language worked on in this unit are:	• understanding telephone messages • writing notes and messages • variations on standard patterns of reported speech • euphemisms and political correctness

Warm-up: Using the phone

Discuss these questions with two or three other students.

a Have you ever spoken English on the telephone?

b If yes, have you had any difficulties either in understanding or in being understood?

c Is it more difficult to speak to someone face to face or to speak to someone on the phone? Give reasons for your answer.

Listening: Advice line

There are a large number of advice lines in Britain which people with all kinds of physical, psychological and practical problems can call in order to listen to some advice. What they hear has been recorded. You are going to listen to one such advice line.

1 The advice line that you are going to listen to is aimed at people who want advice because they feel lonely. What advice do you think you are likely to hear?

2 🔊 Listen to the tape and follow these instructions.

1 Take notes on what you hear.
2 Compare your notes with those made by a partner. Did you hear what you predicted in Exercise 1? Do you think the advice given was sound?

3 Listen again looking at the tapescript on page 171 and underline any words or expressions whose meaning you would like to check.

4 Use a dictionary to check the meanings of anything you underlined.

Writing: Notes and messages

1 Some English friends have asked you to listen to their answerphone and note down any messages while they are on holiday.

Complete a message memo for each of the five messages you listen to. Just note the important information; don't write full sentences.

Call from: ....
For: ....
Message: ....
....
....
....

Call from: ....
For: ....
Message: ....
....
....
....

Call from: ....
For: ....
Message: ....
....
....
....

Call from: ....
For: ....
Message: ....
....
....
....

Call from: ....
For: ....
Message: ....
....
....
....

2 Compare the notes which you wrote with those done by your teacher in response to Exercise 1. Have you included any unnecessary words and phrases? Note how pronouns, auxiliary verbs and other small grammar words, like articles, are often not necessary in notes.

3 Here are some common situations where people need to write a note or a message in English. Working with a partner, write two or three sentences for a card you might give in each of these situations.

a with a present for a friend who has just had a baby
b to a teacher who is retiring from school
c to a friend who has just passed a driving test
d to a friend who has just failed an exam
e to the parents of a friend whom you stayed with last night when you missed your bus home
f to a friend who is not at home when you call (unplanned) to see her
g to a neighbour who has a lot of noisy parties late at night
h to some friends who have just moved into a new house

4 Can you think of some other situations where you have had to write a note or a message recently in your own language? Would you be able to write this note in English? Discuss with other students if you are not sure how it should be done.

Grammar: Variations on standard reported speech

You can either report what someone said by using their exact words and quotation marks or you can use a reporting verb and indirect speech. For example, you can say *'I love you,' he murmured* or *He murmured that he loved her.* The first exercise below revises 'standard' reported speech, which involves a backward shift of tenses in the reported clauses. Later exercises practise other ways of dealing with reported speech in English.

1 Here are some quotations about the telephone. Put them into reported speech using the verbs suggested.

Remember that you usually have to make changes to the original tenses used and that it may be necessary to make some other changes as well.

'Remember that as a teenager you are in the last stage of your life when you will be happy to hear that the phone is for you.'
The American journalist, Fran Lebowitz, warned the boy that ......
....

'My sole inspiration is a telephone call from a director.'
The American composer, Cole Porter, insisted ....
....
....

'Well, if I called the wrong number, why did you answer the phone?'
The American humorist, James Thurber, asked the woman ....
....

'Some women can't see a telephone without taking the receiver off.'
The novelist, Somerset Maugham, claimed ....
....

'If I'm such a legend, then why am I so lonely? If I'm such a legend, then why do I sit at home for hours staring at the damned telephone, hoping it's out of order, even calling the operator asking her if she's sure it's not out of order?'
The US film star, Judy Garland, wondered ....
....
....
....

2 Here are some more verbs which, like *insisted*, *claimed* and *maintained*, for example, are often used when reporting what someone said. Match the verb on the left with the appropriate definition on the right.

assert	agree that something is correct
boast	let something previously secret be known
concede	say something indirectly
confirm	speak very proudly of something you've done
doubt	say something in passing
foresee	say something with conviction
imply	make a solemn promise
mention	admit something reluctantly
reveal	be uncertain about something
vow	predict

3 Choose the most appropriate of the verbs in Exercise 2 and put the statements into reported speech, using *that* clauses and putting the verbs into the necessary tenses. You may need to make some other changes to the original statements as well.

a Whatever happens, I shall always love you, Pete.
Jean ....

b I'm the cleverest person I know.
John ....

c By the way, I saw Sue last night.
Robert ....

d I feel sure there will be trouble if we employ Bill again.
The manager ....

e I suppose Anna's not too bad at arithmetic.
The teacher ....

f You're the first person to know this but I have just finished a novel.
The film star ....

g I don't suppose Jack will win the election.
His brother ....

h Dick, shall we say, didn't always tell the whole truth.
The teacher ....

i Your tickets are in order and your flight will be leaving at 6.30.
The travel agent ....

j Boys are no better at computing than girls – if girls are given the opportunities that boys usually have.
Jane ....

4 You may well find that native speakers do not always follow the rules you have been taught. You may well hear, for instance:

I said I'm coming with you
or:
He promised he'll mend the fence this weekend.

When is it possible to ignore the rules about tense shift when reporting speech?

Look at the following examples.

a The Prime Minister said that his party is more united now than it has ever been.

b Only 21% said they always wash their hands before meals.

c A spokesman for the bank said that very few people will be affected by the change in regulations.

d Mr Menace announced that the company is now making a profit.

e I just told you I've mended it.

What tense would you expect in the reported clauses above?

Why do you think a different tense is possible in the examples?

5 Sometimes you may find that part of a report uses a time shift and part does not. Look at these two sentences. Both are correct but they create a slightly different impression. What is it?

a The company's director said that his intention is still to preserve jobs but that that might involve a reduction in wages for some staff.

b The company's director said that his intention was still to preserve jobs but that that may involve a reduction in wages for some staff.

6 Look again at the sentences you wrote in Exercise 3. Which of them might well be written, or said, without a tense shift?

7 The reporting verb (*say, insist*, etc.) is also sometimes used in the present tense even when it is not making a general statement that is still true. For example, *Everyone agrees that Mr Bloggs is an excellent teacher.* Why do you think the reporting verb can be in the present tense in these examples?

a The author claims that Shakespeare's plays were, in fact, written by Francis Bacon.

b The report argues that the losses were due to mismanagement.

c Mrs Goggins has just phoned and she insists that she wasn't upset by what Pat said.

d Then Jill asks me if I'll speak to him and I say I won't.

8 Read this extract from the novel *The Swimming Pool Season* by Rose Tremain. The novel is about Miriam and her husband, Larry, who go to live in a French village after Larry's swimming pool business fails. Miriam, who paints watercolours and is soon to have an exhibition of her work in Oxford, returns to England to visit her mother, Leni, who is ill. In this extract she is with her grown-up son, Thomas, who runs a furniture business in London, after visiting Leni.

Rewrite it using reported speech. Use some of the verbs and some of the 'non-standard' patterns of tenses that we have looked at in this unit.

'How do you think she was?' asks Miriam, driving to Rothersmere Road.

'Starving.'

'It'll set her back.'

'Yes. Why isn't she fed?'

'I mean the broken ankle. It'll be months before she's well now.'

'So, what are you going to do?'

'Do you mean, will I stay on?'

'Yes.'

'Till the exhibition. Then we'll have to see.'

'Bet Dad's in a mess without you. Can't order a sandwich in French, can he?'

'Oh, he does very well, really. He's picked a lot up.'

'Does he like it?'

'What?'

'France.'

Miriam brings the car to a stop behind the rusting Mini. With dry lips, she says, 'You look pale, Thomas. Why don't you and Perdita come out and stay next summer? Then you can see it all for yourself.'

'You didn't answer my question.'

'I can't.'

'No? Why?'

'If he can get the pool company going again, I think he'll like that.'

'He won't though, will he?'

'Why do you say that?'

'I don't know. No reason.'

Miriam sighs. 'Time will tell,' she says as they get out of the car.

Vocabulary: Euphemisms and political correctness

English people don't like to talk directly about a number of subjects which are felt to be rather difficult in some way; they hesitate before mentioning directly such things as death, for example. They prefer to use expressions which make the difficult topic sound slightly less so. Thus, you will often hear *I'm afraid her granny passed on last night* rather than *I'm afraid her granny died last night*.

The use of a particular kind of euphemism is currently referred to as political correctness or being PC. These are expressions which relate to people and society, and political correctness is a concern not to use language that might be perceived as offensive by particular members of society. Thus, the term *people with learning difficulties* was felt to be better than *mentally handicapped* and the phrase *senior citizens* was preferred to *old age pensioners*. The quotation below illustrates the changing ways in which poverty has been publicly referred to.

I used to think I was poor. Then they told me I wasn't poor, I was needy. Then they told me it was self-defeating to think of myself as needy, I was deprived. Then they told me deprived was a bad image, I was underprivileged. Then they told me underprivileged was overused, I was disadvantaged. I still don't have a dime. But I sure have a great vocabulary.

(Jules Feifer)

1 There were three examples of euphemisms in the telephone messages which you listened to at the beginning of the unit. What were they?

2 Here are some difficult topics which English people often use euphemisms for.

birth   prison   crime
unemployment   lying
toilets   alcohol   warfare
strikes   obesity

Match them to the sentences and decide what the sentences really mean in straightforward English.

a Jill's got a bit of a spare tyre these days, hasn't she?
b Their TV fell off the back of a lorry.
c When is the happy event going to be?
d Would you like to wash your hands?
e Her aunt's a guest of Her Majesty for six months.
f My cousin's an actor but he's resting at the moment.
g The politician seemed to be rather tired and emotional during the debate.
h Pat's being rather economical with the truth, wouldn't you agree?
i The trade union is organising a day of action tomorrow.
j There were three hundred casualties in yesterday's battle for control of the pass.

3 Match the euphemism on the left with what it stands for on the right.

an approved school	financial trouble
cash flow problems	spying organisations
smalls	in the habit of stealing
to have a liquid lunch	to lock someone up (in prison or a mental hospital)
to drown one's sorrows	to drink a lot of alcohol in the middle of the day
light-fingered	underwear
intelligence agencies	a penal institution for minors
the oldest profession	to get drunk
cuddly	prostitution
to put away	fat

4 Some expressions, introduced for PC reasons, have become part of standard English now. Which do you think is the more PC expression in each case? Why?

a an unmarried mother or a single parent?
b children with special needs or educationally subnormal children?
c a housewife or a homemaker?
d Third World countries or developing countries?
e a refuse collector or a dustman?
f a fireman or a firefighter?
g African-American or Black American?
h hearing-impaired or deaf?
i slum or substandard housing?

5 Sometimes political correctness goes to such extremes to avoid hurting others' feelings that it verges on the ridiculous, creating expressions that are excessively convoluted.

Can you match the PC expressions on the left with their translations on the right?

charm-free	bald
nontraditionally ordered	old
chronologically gifted	tall
cosmetically different	boring
hair disadvantaged	disorganised
vertically inconvenienced	stupid
mentally challenged	ugly

6 Now can you work out what the rather extreme PC speaker is saying about the different people below?

a Jack is temporally challenged.
b Jane is a larger than the average citizen.
c Jason is a child with an attention deficit disorder.
d Brian is a person of differing sobriety.
e My mother is an unwaged domestic artist.
f Sue achieved a deficiency on her driving needs assessment.

7 Does your own language also use euphemisms? Can you think of any examples similar to the ones in any of the above exercises?

Six Dinner Sid
Children's stories

The main aspects of language worked on in this unit are:	• reading children's stories • reading aloud • 'unusual' conditionals • collocations • making your own exercises

Warm-up: Talking to children

Discuss the following questions with two or three other students.

a Do you know any children whose first language is English?

b Do you think it can be useful to practise speaking English to children? Why or why not?

c Did you enjoy listening to stories when you were a child? Can you remember any of your favourite stories? If so, tell the other students in your group what you remember about them.

Listening: Children's stories

Look at the illustrations below from a children's book, called *Six Dinner Sid.* What do you think the book will be about?

▭ Now listen to the story about Sid the cat.

Reading: Six Dinner Sid

1 Match the pictures on the previous page to the appropriate parts of the story below.

Sid lived at number one, Aristotle Street.

He also lived at number two, number three, number four, number five and number six.

Sid lived in six houses so that he could have six dinners. Each night he would slip out of number one, where he might have had chicken, into number two for fish, on to number three for lamb, mince at number four, fish again at number five, rounding off at number six with beef and kidney stew.

Since the neighbours did not talk to one another on Aristotle Street, they did not know what Sid was up to. They all believed the cat they fed was theirs and theirs alone.

But Sid had to work hard for his dinners. It wasn't easy being six people's pet. He had six different names to remember and six different ways to behave.

When he was being Scaramouche, Sid put on swanky airs. As Bob he had a job.

He was naughty as Satan and silly as Sally.

As Sooty he smooched but as Schwartz he had to act rough and tough.

All this work sometimes wore Sid out. But he didn't care, as long as he had his six dinners. And besides he liked being scratched in six different places and sleeping in six different beds.

In fact, life in Aristotle Street was just about perfect for Sid until one cold damp day he caught a nasty cough.

The next thing he knew he was being taken to the vet. Poor Sid, he was taken not once, not twice but six times. He went with six different people in six different ways.

The vet said Sid's cough wasn't nearly as nasty as it sounded; but, to be on the safe side, he should have a spoonful of medicine. Of course, Sid didn't have just one spoonful of medicine. He had six.

Now one black cat does look much like another, but nobody, not even a busy vet, could see the same cat six times without becoming suspicious. Sure enough, when he checked in his appointment book, the vet found six cats with a cough – all living in Aristotle Street!

So he rang the owners at once and, oh dear, Sid was found out! When they discovered what he had been up to, Sid's owners were furious. They said he had no business eating so many dinners. They said, in the future, he would have only one dinner a day. But Sid was a six-dinner-a-day cat.

So he went to live at number one, Pythagoras Place.

He also went to live at numbers two, three, four, five and six. Unlike Aristotle Street, the people who lived on Pythagoras Place talked to their neighbours.

So, right from the start, everyone knew about Sid's six dinners. And, because everyone knew, nobody minded.

2 Answer these questions.

a If you were publishing this story, would you ask the artist to draw Aristotle Street with the same kind of houses as Pythagoras Place? Why or why not?

b If there were a picture to match Sid as Scaramouche, Bob, Satan, Sally, Sooty and Schwartz (to go with the lines from *When he was being Scaramouche … to … rough and tough*) what would Sid be doing in each of these roles?

c Describe three other pictures you would ask the artist to draw to illustrate other parts of the story.

3 Discuss these questions with a partner.

a This story is aimed at young children, aged 3 to 5, perhaps. In what ways does this affect the language? Think about vocabulary, structures and any other aspects of style.

b Do you think adults reading this story to children might enjoy it too? Why (not)?

c The story could be seen as having a moral at the end. What is this? Does this affect the appeal of the story?

Speaking: Reading aloud

1 Imagine you are reading aloud to a small child. How does this affect the way you read? Practise reading the story in this way.

If possible, find some other young children's stories and read them aloud – to real English-speaking children, if you can.

2 Answer these questions.

a What is different about reading aloud to other adults as opposed to reading to children?

b When do people need to read aloud to other adults – in English or in your own language? Try to think of half a dozen different situations.

c Reading aloud is quite an art. Most people, naturally, read quite well for children but are less effective at reading for adults. Why do you think this might be the case?

3 Work with a partner and write down five or six tips for people who want to learn to read aloud in a more effective way.

Compare your rules with those devised by other students.

4 Reading aloud can be useful when you are learning a foreign language. Why do you think that reading a poem aloud can be especially appropriate?

5 ▭ Practise reading this poem aloud. Follow these instructions.

1 First make sure that you understand the poem. Read it through, listening to the tape at the same time, and discuss anything you are not sure about. Look any difficult words up in a dictionary.

2 Read the poem aloud, remembering the tips you discussed in Exercise 3. If possible make a recording of your reading. Listen to your recording and redo it, if necessary, until you are absolutely satisfied with your work.

THE LION

The lion just adores to eat
A lot of red and tender meat,
And if you ask the lion what
Is much the tenderest of the lot,
He will not say a roast of lamb
Or curried beef or devilled ham
Or crispy pork or corned beef hash
Or sausages or mutton mash.
Then could it be a big plump hen?
He answers no. What is it, then?
Oh, lion dear, could I not make
You happy with a lovely steak?
Could I entice you from your lair
With rabbit pie or roasted hare?
The lion smiled and shook his head.
He came up very close and said,
'The meat I am about to chew
Is neither steak nor chops. IT'S YOU.'

by Roald Dahl (from *Dirty Beasts*)

Vocabulary: Collocations

Whenever you read something in English, you learn something, consciously or unconsciously, about collocations or words that have a close association with each other.

1 Without looking back at either of the texts, fill in the words in the blanks below.

a When he was being Scaramouche, Sid .... swanky airs.

b One cold damp day he .... a .... cough.

c To be on the .... side, he should have a spoonful of medicine.

d They said he had no .... eating so many dinners.

e They said they would .... sure he had only one dinner a day.

f The lion just adores to eat a lot of red and .... meat.

g The lion smiled and .... his head.

2 Look in your dictionary and find three other collocations to match each of the words below. Write them in the appropriate column.

put on	catch	nasty	safe	business	make	tender	shook

3 Compare the collocations you wrote with those chosen by other students. Add to your lists any other ones which you particularly liked.

4 Write a short story for children using as many of the collocations you have listed as possible.

Read another student's short story – and read it as well as you can – to other students in the class.

Grammar: Unusual conditionals

Here are examples of the four standard conditional patterns:

- If Sid doesn't have six dinners every day, he feels weak.
- If Sid leaves Pythagoras Place, all his new owners will miss him.
- If Sid left Pythagoras Place, all his new owners would miss him.
- If Sid were my cat, I'd be happy for him to eat at the neighbours'.
- If Sid had not kept his lifestyle a secret, his Aristotle Street owners would not have been so angry.

1 Complete the table about the four basic types of conditional exemplified above.

Type	Tense – main clause	Tense – subordinate clause	When used
zero	present		
first		future	
second			to talk about a situation that is (a) hypothetical or (b) very unlikely
third			

2 Now look at these more unusual conditional patterns and try to answer the questions about them.

Variations on the basic patterns

a What is the difference in implication between these two sentences?

   i If I were to read you another story, would you then go to bed quickly?

   ii If I read you one more story, would you then go to bed quickly?

b What is the difference in implication between these two sentences?

   i If Rosa should get the job she's applied for, we would all miss her here.

   ii If Rosa got the job she's applied for, we'd all miss her here.

c Are people more likely to choose to form a conditional sentence by using inversion when speaking or when writing? For example:

   Were Rose to get a new job, we would all miss her here.

   Should the queen abdicate, her eldest son would succeed her.

   Were I a member of the royal family, I'd get pretty annoyed with the press too.

   Had the Prime Minister been totally honest at the outset, the electorate would have been more inclined to support his party.

Variations on the normal sequence of tenses

a When is it possible to form a conditional sentence with two simple past tenses? For example:

   If the weather was damp and cold, my grandmother usually caught a nasty cough.

   If anything got broken at home, it was always John who was to blame.

b When is it possible to have *will* in both clauses? For example:

   I will help you write your dissertation if you will do this translation for me.

   The police will never catch the thieves even if they will set up a special unit to catch them out.

c Similarly, when is it possible to have *would* in both clauses? For example:

   I would be happy to sleep on the floor if you would just let me have some blankets.

   Jane would usually get one of her sisters to do the dirty work if they would be prepared to help her.

d When is it possible to have a verb form associated with the third conditional in one clause and a verb form associated with the second conditional in the other? For example:

   I wouldn't have resigned from my job if I didn't need to go for a higher salary.

   If he didn't take pleasure in preparing special meals, Joe wouldn't have organised so many dinner parties.

   Sam wouldn't be working for Lye Brothers now if his previous boss hadn't been prepared to give him a rather exaggerated reference.

   If we had been born in the nineteenth century, we wouldn't have the chance to travel so widely.

3 Complete the following conditional sentences in any way you like:

a If you will make dinner …
b Were the present government to win the next election …
c Had I known …
d If you should see the manager …
e If it were to rain tomorrow …
f Should the monarch decide to abdicate …

4 Conditional sentences do not always use *if*. They can also use *unless, providing, provided (that), supposing/suppose, on condition (that), as/so long as, say, otherwise*.

Match these expressions with their definitions in the right-hand column.

unless	only if
providing/provided	if not
supposing/suppose	if not
on condition	imagine
as/so long as	imagine
say	only if
otherwise	only if

5 Complete the sentences below in any logical way.

a I won't lend you the money unless …
b I'll lend you my car provided …
c Supposing you were offered the job …
d We'll do what you ask as long as …
e So long as … I shan't mind what you do.
f Providing … you can buy what you like.
g They'll give us the papers on condition that …
h She refused to work late unless …
i Say he …, would you still want to marry him?
j I'm glad I found out that the flight had been cancelled. Otherwise, …
k Suppose they asked you to do something dishonest, …
l … . Otherwise, you'll be very late.

6 Practise writing some conditional sentences about students in your class. Fill the main blanks in the sentences below with the name of any student in the class. Then complete the sentences in any appropriate way.

a .... could become a successful politician provided …
b .... won't succeed in life unless …
c Supposing the teacher …, ... would be very happy.
d Say .... …, we would all be proud of him/her.
e .... might become world famous on condition that …

Compare your sentences with those written by other students.

Study skills: Making your own exercises

Make some exercises for the other students in this class revising the two previous units which you have worked on. Work with a partner and follow the instructions to prepare three exercises.

1 Write a vocabulary exercise where students have to match ten words or expressions with their definitions – choose any words and expressions you think are useful.
2 Prepare a grammar exercise where students have to fill in blanks in ten sentences to practise the grammar points you are focusing on.

3 Select some useful words or expressions from work you have done recently in class or at home. Put them in sentences of your own, underlining the word or expression you are dealing with. The other students have to explain what the underlined word or expression means.

Make sure you keep a separate note of the answers to your exercises.

Exchange your exercises with those prepared by other students.

Writing the exercises as well as doing them will help you to revise work recently done.

Let's take a closer look
Tourist guides

The main
aspects of
language
worked on in
this unit are:

- listening to tourist guides
- taking notes
- more on prepositions
- homophones

Warm-up: A tourist sight

Look at the pictures. Describe them in as much detail as you can.

Listening: Tourist guides

1 ▭ Listen to the tour. Which of the photos shows a place visited on the tour? Write phrases beside that photo to give more information about what the photo shows.

2 ▭ Listen again and take notes on what you hear. Compare your notes with those made by two other students. Which of you has taken the fullest notes? Check with the teacher or other students if there are any points where your notes do not agree.

3 Here are some words used by the tourist guides. Use them to make sentences about Trinity College – you may change the form of the word if you wish.

a landowner	**c** merge	**e** insignia	**g** sceptre
b found	**d** armour	**f** blank	**h** gravity

4 Answer these questions.

a Which two historical figures do you hear impersonated on the tape?
b What is suggested about the character of the first of these figures?
c What is the piece of folklore connecting the second figure with the college today?

Writing: Note-taking

1 When might it be useful for you to be able to take good notes –
either in your own language or in English – when listening to
someone? Try to think of at least three situations when you
might need to take notes.

2 Answer these questions.   **a** When you take notes, how can the following help you?

> abbreviations   punctuation   initials   numbered points
> drawings

b Do you have any special devices that you personally find useful
when taking notes? If so, explain them to the other students in
the class.

3 Here are some abbreviations, signs and symbols
which you may find useful when taking notes in
English. Explain what each of them means and
write each in an appropriate context.

a e.g.	**e** c. 500 people	**i** =
b etc.	**f** Shakespeare et al.	**j** <
c N.B.	**g** →	**k** >
d 15th c.	**h** ∴	**l** &

4 Here is a text written in note form. Expand the notes into full
sentences. The text is about Lady Margaret Beaufort who was a
very influential woman in 15th-century England. Born into one
of the most important families in the country, she had three
husbands (all men of consequence) and founded two colleges
in Cambridge.

> *Lady Margaret Beaufort. b. 1443*
> *= d. of Sir John Beaufort, 1st Duke of Somerset*
> *= m. of Henry VII (b. 1457)*
> *1455 (!) married Edmund Tudor*
> *During part of Wars of Roses (1455–85, betw.*
> *Houses of Lancaster & York) MB imprisoned at*
> *Pembroke by Yorkists.*
> *Lancastrian claim to Eng. throne passed to MB*
> *as grand-d. of John of Gaunt (after extinction*
> *of male line)*
> *Henry ascended throne after defeat Richard III*
> *1485 (Battle of Bosworth Field)*
> *1464 m. 2 Henry Stafford (s. of Duke of*
> *Buckingham)*
> *1475 m. 3 Thomas Stanley (1st Earl of Derby)*
> *Founded Christ's and St John's Colls., Camb.*
> *Endowed 2 divinity professorships at Oxford*
> *& Cambridge*
> *Patron of Will. Caxton (1st Eng. printer)*
> *d. 1509*

5 The text below is about the state of Britain in 1485 but it is written in the style of a contemporary newspaper article. Follow these instructions.

1 Read the text. What features of the language indicate that it was supposedly written in 1485?
2 Write notes on it. Make use of the following in your notes where possible – abbreviations, punctuation, initials and numbered points.

Three Centuries of Plantagenet Rule Draw to a Close

British Isles, 1485

OF THE MANY CHANGES that have taken place in 300 years of Plantagenet rule in England, one of the most significant has been the slow erosion of French influence. Nearly all the lands in France that were once held by English kings have now been lost. French used to be the language of both the court and the cultured elite – Henry IV (1399–1413) was the first king after the Conquest of 1066 whose mother tongue was English – but now the native language is gaining a new respectability.

Scotland, beyond the writ of Plantagenet kings but well within the scope of their ambitions, has grown since the 12th century into a far more united kingdom than it had been previously. The Scots have also managed to fight off English encroachments on their independence. Life here is distinguished by an openness towards continental (particularly French) influences, in both trade and culture.

The Welsh came close to maintaining their own independence from the Plantagenets, but the Glyndwr rebellion, which was crushed at the beginning of this century, changed all that. Now Wales is forced into getting the best that it can within the framework of English politics. It may be some small consolation that the new king, Henry Tudor (Twdwr) is a quarter Welsh. Ireland has changed radically since Henry II of England's invasion in 1171. The country is now effectively split into two parts. There is the 'Englishry' which is itself effectively divided into that region where Anglo-Irish lords hold territories in fief from the English king and another of more direct English rule known as 'the Pale', centred on Dublin. There is the 'Irishry' comprising most of the north and west of the country, where Gaelic lords still rule according to Irish custom.

6 ▭ Listen to the next part of the tape taking tourists round Cambridge. Make notes on what you hear. Look at your notes and talk about Christ's College.

7 Follow these instructions to become a tourist guide for the rest of the class.

1 If possible, look in an English encyclopedia. Look up a famous town or other place in your country or elsewhere. Alternatively, just look up your own country or another one that interests you. Make notes on what you read.
2 If you do not have access to an encyclopedia in English, look up a place in your own language, but make notes on the entry in English.
3 Imagine you are a tourist guide for the place you have researched. Looking at your notes, tell the tourists (the other members of your class) about your place.

Grammar: Prepositions

1 ▭ Try to fill in the prepositions in these extracts from the tape without listening to the tape again. Then listen and correct your work.

a You should now be standing .... point 18 .... the cobbled area .... Trinity College.

b .... the Royal Family and the Church, Trinity is the largest institutional landowner .... England.

c The college is steeped .... history and tradition.

d It was founded .... King Henry VIII.

e Rather than starting .... scratch, he merged two existing colleges.

f This gatehouse was built .... the 1490s and was originally the gatehouse .... one .... the merged colleges, King's Hall.

g The third .... the left denotes Edward the Black Prince who got his nickname .... the unusual black colour .... his battle armour.

h .... it, you can see the white feathers which were his insignia .... the Prince .... Wales.

i And there's an interesting story .... the shield on the right.

j Don't be surprised if you've never heard .... him.

k Some students removed the original sceptre and replaced it .... a chair leg.

l I wonder what Henry would have thought .... that.

m If I wasn't stuck .... here, I'd have the lot of them arrested and put .... the Tower.

n They should have their heads cut .... I did it .... two of my six wives, you know.

o .... the middle of the lawn .... the right is an apple tree.

p This is part .... college folklore which relates .... one .... its most famous students.

q It was the sight .... an apple falling .... a tree that set Newton thinking .... the theory .... gravity.

r This tree is reputed to have grown .... a seed .... that same tree that grew .... Newton's garden.

2 Now look at the picture of Christ's College. Write a detailed description of it, describing carefully where things are. Think especially carefully about the prepositions you use.

3 Here is another text from the book of supposedly contemporary news articles; this one is about the execution of Anne Boleyn, Henry VIII's second wife. Each blank indicates that a preposition is missing. Fill in the missing prepositions.

Anne Loses Her Head

London, 19th May 1536

THE EXECUTIONER'S SWORD glinted (1) .... the morning sun, as Anne Boleyn was brought (2) .... the block today. Escorted (3) .... four ladies-in-waiting, the queen, dressed (4) .... grey, climbed the scaffold and faced the French swordsman whose services she had specifically requested. The beheading, it is reported, was swift and efficient, requiring only one stroke (5) .... the sword.

The charge (6) .... the queen and Lord Rochford, her brother, was one (7) .... treason. They were accused (8) .... attempting to hasten Henry VIII's death (9) .... their incestuous liaison. Four other men have already lost their heads (10) .... alleged adultery (11) .... the queen. A tribunal, headed (12) .... Anne's uncle, the Duke (13) .... Norfolk, found both guilty and the sentences (14) .... death were passed.

Anne appeared resigned (15) .... her fate, even praising Henry (16) .... the last. 'I pray God save the king and send him long to reign (17) .... you, for a gentler, nor a more merciful prince was there never, and (18) .... me he was ever a good, a gentle and a sovereign lord.'

Vocabulary: Homophones

English is very rich in homophones or words which have the same pronunciation but different spellings and different meanings. Think of the word /saɪt/ for instance. It can be written *sight*, *site* and *cite*. Do you know what all these mean?

1 Look again at either the text about the British Isles in 1485 or the one about the execution of Anne Boleyn. Find five examples of homophones in the text you chose. Write each example down with its alternative spelling(s), e.g. *their/there/they're*.

2 Follow these instructions.

1 Write down twelve more sets of English homophones? Write them down with both of their spellings, e.g. *tail, tale*. Do not count any practised in the previous exercise.

2 Compare the ones you wrote with those thought of by other students in the class. How many did the class as a whole (hole!) find (fined!)? List them all on the board (bored!).

3 Choose some of the words from the board that you would particularly like to learn. Write them down in the context of a sentence.

3 Look at these pairs of sentences. In each pair, the blanks can be filled by a word that sounds the same. What are the words which fit each pair of sentences?

a i What can we do to .... John's spirits – he seems so depressed at the moment?

ii The sun's .... are particularly strong at midday when they are at their shortest.

b i Every Sunday in church we would begin by singing a ....

ii I like her but I really can't stand ....

c i Put the video on ....; I want to have a look at that actor in the background.

ii Look at the cat, licking its .... so delicately.

d i Those knives are made of stainless ...., not silver.

ii At least my bike's so old that no one would ever want to .... it.

e i I'm only telling you this because I know you are very .... and won't pass it on.

ii Every class you teach somehow has its own .... identity.

f i Whoopi Goldberg pretended to be a .... in the film *Sister Act*.

ii .... of the food we prepared was actually eaten.

g i She was expelled from school because she .... her hair blue.

ii He .... two years ago today.

h i .... is a small country to the west of England.

ii .... are the largest sea mammals.

4 Make an exercise like Exercise 3 for other students in the class. Write gapped sentences for the pair or set of homophones which your teacher gives you. When you are ready, try your exercise on other students.

The main aspects of language worked on in this unit are:

- reading letters
- punctuation
- the perfect forms of the verb
- study skills – problem-solving

Warm-up: About letters

Discuss these questions with two or three other students.

a How often do you write and receive letters?

b Tell each other about the most recent letter you wrote and the most recent one you received. How did you feel reading or writing these letters?

c Can you remember any particularly special letters you have received? Why were they special?

d Can you remember any letters that you took particular trouble over writing? Why did you make a particular effort with these letters?

e Are there people whose letters you particularly enjoy receiving? Why are their letters special?

f How do you think the use of (a) faxes and (b) e-mail will affect people's letter-writing habits?

Reading: Letters

1 Read the extracts from three rather unusual letters below. For each one, discuss these questions with a partner.

a What do you learn about the writer and their relationship with the person they are writing to? Why did the writer write the letter?

b How do you think the recipient felt on getting the letter? Why?

May 8th 1872

Darling Child,

I am most thankful to hear you are going on so satisfactorily. I never thought you cared (having three of each) whether it was a son or daughter; indeed I think many Princes a great misfortune – for they are in one another's and almost everybody's way. I am sure it is the case here – and dear Papa felt this so much that he was always talking of establishing if possible one or two of your brothers and eventual grandchildren (of which I fear there is the prospect of a legion with but little money) in the colonies. I don't dislike babies, though I think very young ones rather disgusting, and I take an interest in those of my children when they are two or three – and of people who are dear to me and whom I am fond of – but when they come at the rate of three a year it becomes a cause of mere anxiety for my own children and of no great interest. What name is this fourth daughter to have?

October 2nd, 1848

My Dear Sir,

'We have buried our dead out of sight.' A lull begins to succeed the gloomy tumult of last week. It is not permitted us to grieve for him who is gone as others grieve for those they lose. The removal of our only brother must necessarily be regarded by us rather in the light of a mercy than a chastisement. Branwell was his father's and his sisters' pride in boyhood, but since manhood, the case has been otherwise. It has been our lot to see him take a wrong bent; to hope, expect, wait his return to the right path; to know the sickness of hope deferred, the dismay of prayer baffled; to experience despair at last – and now to observe the sudden early obscure close of what might have been a noble career.

I do not weep from a sense of bereavement – there is no prop withdrawn, no consolation torn away, no dear companion lost – but for the wreck of talent, the ruin of promise, the untimely dreary extinction of what might have been a burning and a shining light. My brother was a year my junior. I had aspirations and ambitions for him once, long ago – they have perished mournfully. Nothing remains of him but a memory of errors and sufferings. There is such a bitterness of pity for his life and death, such a yearning for the emptiness of his whole existence as I cannot describe. I trust time will allay these feelings.

My poor father naturally thought more of his *only* son than of his daughters, and, much and long as he had suffered on his account, he cried out of his loss like David for that of Absalom, – my son!, my son! – and refused at first to be comforted…

My unhappy brother never knew what his sisters had done in literature – he was not aware that they had ever published a line. We could not tell him of our efforts for fear of causing him too deep a pang of remorse for his own time misspent, and talents misapplied. Now he will *never* know. I cannot dwell longer on the subject at present – it is too painful.

I thank you for your kind sympathy, and pray earnestly that your sons may all do well, and that you may be spared the sufferings my father has gone through.

Yours sincerely,

C Brontë

New Cross,
Hatcham,
Surrey

I love your verses with all my heart, dear Miss Barrett – and this is no off-hand complimentary letter that I shall write – whatever else, no prompt matter-of-course recognition of your genius, and there a graceful and natural end of the thing: since the day last week when I first read your poems, I quite laugh to remember how I have been turning and turning again in my mind what I should be able to tell you of their effect upon me – for in the first flush of delight I thought I would this once get out of my habit of purely passive enjoyment, when I do really enjoy, and thoroughly justify my admiration – perhaps even, as a loyal fellow-craftsman should, try and find fault and do you some little good to be proud of hereafter! – but nothing comes of it at all – so into me has it gone, and part of me has it become, this great living poetry of yours. I do, as I say, love these books with all my heart – and I love you too: do you know I was once not very far from seeing – really seeing you? Mr Kenyon said to me one morning 'Would you like to see Miss Barrett?' – then he went to announce me, – then he returned… you were too unwell – and now it is years ago – and I feel as at some untoward passage in my travels – as if I had been close, so close, to some world's-wonder in chapel or crypt, only a screen to push and I might have entered, but there was some slight… so it now seems… slight and just-sufficient bar to admission; and the half-opened door shut, and I went home my thousands of miles, and the sight was never to be!

Well, these Poems were to be – and this true thankful joy and pride with which I feel myself
Yours ever faithfully,
Robert Browning

2 Read the first letter (from Queen Victoria) again and say whether the following sentences are true or false.

a The writer of this letter would have preferred her daughter to have a son.
b The writer is a widow.
c The writer has not got many grandchildren.
d The writer was only interested in her own children when they were two or three years old.
e The writer likes all older children.
f The writer feels very anxious about her own grandchildren.
g The writer is addressing one of her own sons.
h The addressee already has three children.
i The writer is longing to know the name of her new grandchild.

3 Read the second letter again and answer these questions.

a What do you think might have happened to her brother to destroy his family's dreams?
b What does this letter tell you about the position of women in England in 1848?

4 Read the third letter again. Correct these statements about this letter.

a This is the second time Robert Browning has written to Miss Barrett.
b Robert and Miss Barrett had met once many years ago.
c Robert Browning would have liked to be a poet himself.
d Robert Browning liked Miss Barrett's poems because he was in love with her.

5 Could the message conveyed in each of these letters have been as effectively conveyed over the telephone? Why or why not?

What for you is the most striking characteristic of each of these letters?

Vocabulary: From the texts

1 Follow these instructions.

1 Make a list of six words or expressions that you would particularly like to learn from these letters.
2 Compare the words and expressions you have listed with those selected by another student.
3 Discuss how to write down all the vocabulary items you and your partner have selected in a way that will help you to remember them. Would it be most appropriate, for example, to draw a diagram, write an example sentence, give a translation and/or to use any other methods?
4 Write your words and expressions in the ways you decided upon.

2 Complete the word family table for some of these words from the letters. Remember to use prefixes and suffixes as appropriate.

Noun(s)	Verb(s)	Adjective(s)	Adverb(s)
			satisfactorily
(mis)fortune	–		
	grieve		–
		obscure	
bereavement			–
aspiration(s)			–
		complimentary	
recognition			
delight			
	justify		
pride			
		thankful	

3 Write down three objects which could follow each of these verbs.

For example, *to establish a company, links, trust.*

a to bury   f to spare
b to defer   g to enjoy
c to experience   h to justify
d to observe   i to announce
e to refuse   j to push

4 Look again at the words in Exercise 3 and write down a noun with the same root for each one.

For example, *to establish, establishment.*

Writing: Punctuation

1 **Answer these questions.**

a What are the conventions of punctuating a letter in English – think about the address, the salutation at the beginning and the closing of the letter?

b Which two punctuation marks are especially common in informal letters or notes? Why do you think they are especially common in this kind of writing?

c Do your answers agree with those your teacher has? If not, can you argue the case for your own answers?

2 **Read this nineteenth-century schoolmistress's verse on the rules of punctuation and follow these instructions.**

1 Underline all the names of punctuation marks used in the verse.

2 Decide if all the punctuation rules described in the verse are also illustrated in the verse.

3 Write out the 17 rules presented in the verse. Then write your own sentences – on the subject of spelling in English – to illustrate each of the rules.

Sentences start with a Capital letter,
So as to make your sentences better.
Use a full stop to mark the end.
It closes every sentence penned.
The comma is for short pauses and breaks,
And also for lists the writer makes.
Dashes – like these – are for thoughts by the way.
They give extra information (so do brackets, we may say).
These two dots are a colon: colons pause to compare.
They also do this: list, explain and prepare.
The semicolon makes a break; it's followed by a clause.
It does the work of words that link; it's also a short pause.
An apostrophe shows the owner of anyone's things,
And it's also useful for shortenings.
I'm so glad! He's so mad! We're having such a lark!
To show strong feelings use an exclamation mark!
A question mark follows What? When? Where? Why? and How?
Do you? Can I? Shall we? Give us your answer now!
'Quotation marks' enclose what is said,
Which is why they're sometimes called 'speech marks' instead.

3 **Punctuate the following paragraph.**

punctuation may not be as tightly regulated in English as it is in some other languages but it still has a very important role to play and must be used appropriately if a writer forgets about punctuation his or her work can be very difficult to follow as this paragraph illustrates sometimes moreover different uses of punctuation can affect meaning

4  Listen to the letter on the tape. It was published in *The Times* on 2nd September 1995 in response to a story about students withdrawing their applications for university entrance. Take the letter down as dictation, taking care to use all the necessary punctuation marks and capital letters.

Grammar: Perfect forms of the verb

1 Complete the table with the perfect forms of the verb *to write.*

time	perfect simple	perfect continuous
past present future	had written	

2 The perfect form tells us something about the way the speaker or writer views what he or she is describing. It can serve to give a kind of personal interpretation of events.

Answer the following questions.

a What does the use of the present perfect suggest about an event that the past or present simple does not? (For example, why does Charlotte Brontë say *It has been our lot to see him take a wrong bent* rather than *It was our lot … or It is our lot…*?)

b What does the use of the past perfect rather than the past simple emphasise? (For example, what is the difference between *I'd bought the house two years before we got married* and *I bought the house two years before we got married*?)

c What does the use of the future perfect focus on? (For example, what is the difference in emphasis between *We'll have paid off our mortgage in two years' time* and *We'll pay off our mortgage in two years' time*?)

d Having looked at the different perfect tenses, what do you think is the general significance of the perfect forms of the verb?

e In what ways do the perfect continuous forms differ in meaning or emphasis from the perfect simple forms?

3 Comment on these other uses in the letters you read.

a Why do you think Queen Victoria wrote 'Dear Papa was always talking of establishing one or two of your brothers … in the colonies' rather than 'Dear Papa has always been talking … '?

b Why does she say 'I take an interest in those of my children when they are two or three' rather than 'I have taken an interest … '

c Why does Charlotte Brontë say 'what might have been a noble career' rather than 'what might be a noble career'?

d Why does she say 'My aspirations … have perished mournfully' rather than 'My aspirations … perished mournfully'?

e Why is it 'long as he had suffered on his account' rather than 'long as he suffered on his account'?

f Why does she conclude by referring to 'the sufferings my father has gone through' rather than 'the sufferings my father went through'?

g Why does Robert Browning say 'I quite laugh to remember how I have been turning and turning again in my mind what I should be able to tell you of their effect upon me' rather than 'I quite laugh to remember how I have turned and turned again my mind what I should be able to tell you of their effect upon me'?

h Why does he say 'Part of me has it become, this great living poetry of yours' rather than 'Part of me it became … ' or 'Part of me it becomes … '?

4 All the sentences in the exercise below are correct. Comment on the difference in nuance between the sentences in each set.

a i We've worked on the project for three years.
  ii We worked on the project for three years.
  iii We've been working on the project for three years.

b i Jack had planned to resign when Jill took over.
  ii Jack planned to resign when Jill took over.
  iii Jack had been planning to resign when Jill took over.

c i In June Mary will act as manager for one year.
  ii In June Mary will have acted as manager for one year.
  iii In June Mary will have been acting as manager for one year.

d i Silvia went to New York.
  ii Silvia has gone to New York.
  iii Silvia has been going to New York.
  iv Silvia was going to New York.
  v Silvia has been to New York.

e i Rod's lost weight rapidly.
  ii Rod's losing weight rapidly.
  iii Rod loses weight rapidly.
  iv Rod's been losing weight rapidly.

f i I'll write the letters tomorrow.
  ii I'll be writing the letters tomorrow.
  iii I'll have written the letters tomorrow.
  iv I'll have been writing the letters tomorrow.

5 Follow these instructions.

1 With a partner write some sets of sentences of your own like those in the previous activity.

2 Discuss what effect the changes in verb forms make.

3 Exchange sentences with another pair. Comment on what the difference is between the sentences in their set. Does your interpretation agree with theirs?

Study skills: Problem solving forum

Follow these instructions.

1 Divide into groups of five or six students. Each group is a forum whose aim is to give advice to students with problems.

2 Choose a problem from those below (a–f) – each student should take a different problem. If preferred, you may invent a completely different study problem of your own.

3 Write a brief letter to the forum asking for advice. Expand on the problem given in any way you like. You can write as yourself or you can take on a totally different persona.

4 Someone from each group reads out one of the letters.

5 The forum should then discuss the problem. If they wish, they may ask the student who wrote the letter additional questions. They should then – orally – give as many different pieces of advice as possible. The student presenting the problem should take brief notes on the advice received.

6 This process should be repeated until all the problem letters have been dealt with.

7 Regroup so that the students who wrote about problem similar problems are together. Compare the advice received.

8 Make a poster to put on the classroom wall, summarising the different pieces of advice you received. Any students who worked on problems of their own invention should produce their own individual posters.

9 One person from each group should present the poster to the rest of the class, going through all the points made and expanding on them where necessary.

a I get very nervous before oral exams.

b I find it very hard to learn new vocabulary in English.

c Sometimes I don't feel that I'm making any progress in English. What can I do to make sure that I really am progressing?

d I wish I could get more practice at listening to and speaking English outside the classroom. What can you suggest?

e My teacher has asked me to make a list of all the kinds of reference books which a school library should contain and to say why each of them is useful. What should I put on the list?

f I find it really hard to get down to study outside class. What do you recommend?

The main aspects of language worked on in this unit are:	• listening to snippets of conversation
	• small talk
	• grammar and pronunciation
	• compound nouns

Warm-up: Eavesdropping

1 Answer the following questions.

a What is eavesdropping?
b Do you ever eavesdrop?
c Have you ever heard anything interesting when you've been eavesdropping?

Remember that eavesdropping on English conversations can help you learn!

2 Work in pairs. Discuss the topic which your teacher will give you.

As you talk, the teacher will give some people some special instructions.

Listening: Snippets of conversation

⌨ Listen to the tape. For each conversation answer the following questions:

a What do you think is the relationship between the people who are talking?
b What are they talking about?
c Note one word or phrase which indicated for you what the context of the conversation was.

Complete the table as you listen.

Conversation	Relationship	Topic	Word or phrase
1			
2			
3			
4			
5			
6			
7			
8			
9			
10			
11			
12			

Speaking: Small talk

1 Imagine you are at a formal party with people whom you are meeting for the first time. Which of the subjects below do you think are appropriate as topics for conversation in (a) your own country and (b) Britain? Complete the table below, adding any comments if you wish.

Topic	Own country	Britain
today's weather		
your opinions about marriage		
your religious beliefs		
how you got to the party		
your political views		
a recent sporting event		
the food and drink at the party		
your salary		
a TV programme you saw last night		
the latest political crisis		
the attractiveness of your host		
a neighbour's sudden death		
some physical symptoms you've got		

2 Are these appropriate ways of starting a conversation with someone you don't know at a party?

a Haven't we met somewhere before?
b Do you come here often?
c It's a bit chilly today, isn't it?
d How much did those beautiful shoes cost?
e Can I get you something to drink?
f Where do you work?
g What do you think of the Prime Minister?
h Are you a friend of Jane's?
i Would you like to dance?
j Have you got a light?
k This is a pretty boring party, isn't it?
l How old are you?

Can you suggest any good ways of starting a conversation?

3 Work with a partner. Imagine that you are in one of the locations shown in the illustrations on page 125 and that you have never met each other before. Take it in turns to initiate a conversation and carry on the conversation as seems appropriate to you. When the conversation comes to a natural end, move on to a different location.

4 Follow these instructions.

1 You are going to role play being at a formal party where few of the guests already know each other, a party in an embassy, perhaps.
2 Your teacher will give you a card to describe the character of the person you are to be.
3 Look at your card. How might that person behave at a formal party? What sorts of things would he or she talk about?
4 Act your role. Try to move around the party speaking to as many people as possible.
5 After the role-play, discuss what roles you felt the other students were playing.

Grammar: Pronunciation

Contractions

Normally when we speak, we do not pronounce in full auxiliary verbs with a pronoun or with *not*. We say *I'm* rather than *I am*, for example, unless we are being particularly formal or emphatic for some reason. You are, of course, familiar with the way contractions are formed in English but it is easy to forget to pronounce verbs in the contracted way when you speak.

1 Complete the table with the contracted form of the phrase given. Then write an example sentence illustrating the contraction and using the words *repair* and *car* in some way. The first one is done for you as an example.

Phrase	Contraction	Example sentence
they will	they'll	They'll repair your car for you.
she would		
we had		
it has		
he is		
cannot		
dare not		
might not		
must not		
ought not		
shall not		
will not		
here is		
that will		
what will		
where is		
who will		
who would		
how has		

2 Exchange example sentences with a partner and practise reading each other's sentences.

3 ⌷ Listen to the tape and take down the sentences you hear as dictation.

Emphatic stress on the auxiliary verb

If you wish to say something particularly emphatically, you may do so by giving an unusually strong stress to the auxiliary verb, by saying *I* **am** *paying attention*, for example, instead of the more usual *I'm paying attention*.

If you wish to emphasise a verb in the present or past simple, then you can add *do/does* or *did* and give that a strong stress.

I **do** *love you.*
He **did** *tell the truth.*

4 Say these statements in a particularly emphatic way, adding *do/does/did* where necessary. With a partner put each of the emphatic sentences into a mini-dialogue to show how such an emphatic sentence might be used in practice.

Example:
Mum: *Jane got her exam results today and she's passed everything – even though she said she was sure she'd failed.*
Dad: *That's wonderful! So, Jane* **is** *going to be a teacher.*

a Jane's going to be a teacher.
b She passed her exams.
c She'll find a job quite easily.
d She always wanted to work with children.
e I've seen her teach.
f She teaches well.
g She's a kind person.
h I know her well.
i She'd like to find work in London.
j She understands what is involved in teaching.

Pronunciation of the past simple ending

5 Compare the sounds at the end of the verbs *listened, eavesdropped* and *noted*.

6 Write the past simple forms of these verbs in the appropriate column.

⌷ Check your answers by listening to the pronunciation on the tape.

kick sob fade
approach hug knit
wash watch bath
buzz hop slam walk
miss sunbathe quote
hope / cringe yell
intend love laugh
organise purr line
vow assert try race
stare

Ending /d /	**Ending** /t /	**Ending** /ɪd /

7 What is the rule about how the past tense ending is pronounced?

Add three more verbs to each of the columns.

Pronunciation of *the*

Just as the past simple ending is pronounced differently depending on the sound which precedes it, so *the* is pronounced differently depending on its context.

8 Follow these instructions.

1 🔲 Listen to and say these phrases:

> in the car   bite the apple   ride the bicycle
> listen to the owl   feed the dog
> on the hour   with the uncle
> go to the university   pick the flower

2 Explain what the rule is for how *the* is pronounced.

3 Look at your vocabulary notebook and write down five more examples of phrases using *the* for each of the two different pronunciations. If possible, write down phrases that you have recently learnt.

9 🔲 Listen to these sentences on the tape and explain what is unusual about the pronunciation of *the* in them.

That's the car!
Buy the bike!
It's the house!
That's the ring!

Why do you think the speaker has chosen to say the sentences in this way?

With a partner write a sentence or two describing the context for each sentence.

Example:
You saw a car which you really wanted to buy but you can't afford it. You were telling your friend about it and now you look out of the window and you see it parked on the other side of the street.

10 Say the sentences aloud both in the normal way and in the more emphatic way.

Vocabulary: Compound nouns

Small talk is a compound noun – a fixed expression made up of more than one word and functioning as a noun. There are hundreds of these in English. Other examples from the listening texts are *news room*, *finance department*, *rush hour*.

1 Match the words on the left with those on the right in order to make ten more examples of compound nouns.

bottle	fever
bubble	air
general	tongue
open	barrier
current	public
sound	opener
junk	bath
hay	meter
parking	affairs
mother	food

2 Read this article on the effects of exercise on health from *Time magazine*. Write down all the examples of compound nouns in the article.

NO SWEAT?

Then No Extra Years

HARRIED BUSINESS EXECUTIVES MAY shoehorn an occasional squash game or round of golf into their overscheduled lives. Office clerks may sometimes trade a quick bite for a gym class during lunch hours. But if they want to get more out of their exercise routine than a competitive attitude or a leaner look, they are going to have to step up the pace. At least that is the conclusion of a Harvard study reported last week in the *Journal of the American Medical Association*. The research tracked 17,300 middle-aged men over 20 years and found that those who exercised vigorously lived longer than those who broke a sweat only once or twice a week.

The Harvard study seems certain to sow confusion on America's treadmills and couches. Only two weeks ago a study of 9,777 men reported in the same journal by the Cooper Institute for Aerobics Research, determined that any improvement in fitness translated into longer life. Even couch potatoes could cut their death risk nearly in half if they started walking 3.2 kilometres in 28 to 30 minutes every other day. Earlier the US Centers for Disease Control and Prevention, in conjunction with the American College of Sports Medicine, also trumpeted the health benefits of moderation. When health advice starts to confuse rather than illuminate, a little common sense seems the best course of action. Even if moderate exercise doesn't prolong your life, it improves your quality of life. So the best exercise that you can do probably turns out to be something that you enjoy – whether it's an aerobics workout or just a brief walk. All it takes is getting up from the couch, turning off the TV and striding – briskly – out of the door.

3 Look at each compound noun you wrote down in turn. Can you find another compound noun which uses one of the same parts as the noun in the article.

For example:
business executive – business partner, sales executive

The main aspects of language worked on in this unit are:
- reading reviews
- criticising tactfully
- complex sentences
- topic vocabulary
- what to read in English

Warm-up: Talking about entertainment

1 Follow these instructions.

1 Write the heading FILMS on a blank sheet in your vocabulary notebook.
2 As a class, brainstorm all the words and expressions which you associate with films.
3 Select from all the brainstormed words and expressions those which you wish to learn. Write them down in an appropriate way on the FILMS sheet in your notebook.

2 Think about three or four films, videos or TV programmes that you have recently watched. What did you like and what did you not like about them? Make notes to complete the chart below.

Title	Good points	Bad points

3 Tell a partner about what you wrote in your chart. Explain the notes in your last two columns more fully. Compare opinions with your partner if you have seen the films or programmes your partner chose to comment on.

Reading: Reviews

1 Below and on the next page there are a number of short film reviews. Before reading any of the reviews in full, answer the following questions quickly.

  a Which films are being reviewed?
  b Have you seen any of the films being reviewed?
  c If so, what was your opinion of them?
  d If you haven't seen any of the films, do you already know anything about them? If so, what?

2 Now read the reviews and make notes under these three headings for each film:

  a What facts you learn about the film
  b Good points about it
  c Bad points about it

3 Which tense do the reviewers use when they are describing events in the film? Why do you think they choose this tense rather than, say, the past simple?

4 The first and last sentences of reviews are often written for a special effect – to capture the reader's attention and to leave the reader with a clear impression of the critic's opinion, respectively. Is that the case with the reviews here? If so, in what ways do the critics here make their first and last sentences special?

5 The two longer reviews, those for *The House of the Spirits* and *Jurassic Park*, come from a rather more informal magazine than the other four reviews do. Can you find any examples of particularly informal style from these two reviews?

6 You can rent the video of one of these films to watch in class. Which would you choose?

Shoot the Pianist is widely acknowledged as one of the key films of the French New Wave. Truffaut is typically playful with the conventions of Hollywood film noir, jumping between contrasting moods unexpectedly and tossing in sudden and unpredictable mood twists. Aznavour is excellent as the bar room pianist who gets involved with gangsters, his performance adding greatly to the effects of this blithe homage to the American B-movie.

Hello, I'm Forrest, Forrest Gump. Not much of an opening line, is it? Yet Tom Hanks's portrayal of this sweet, naive Everyman has already made *Forrest Gump* one of Paramount's biggest grossing films to date. Whether the Brits will share the American nostalgic delight as Gump glides, bemused, through America's post-war history remains to be seen. Robert Zemeckis's film is diverting, certainly; it is also around 45 minutes too long.

While Spielberg perhaps wasn't the best person to direct an adaptation of Alice Walker's novel about a poor black woman's life of hardship in the Deep South, he was probably one of the few directors with the clout to bring such material into the Hollywood mainstream. Though flawed, the film of *The Color Purple* features a number of outstanding performances, while the compelling power of the original material often transcends Spielberg's overly sentimental treatment.

A hip, gaudy and brash re-telling of the panto favourite for the switched-on MTV generation, *Aladdin* eschews depth and character development for pace and raw energy. Though filled with dazzling effects, the film's trump card is Robin Williams whose mercurial genie kicks the film into overdrive with his flipped-out chatter. Disney's animators have matched Williams's stream of consciousness ramblings image for image, giving new meaning to the phrase 'quick on the draw'. If *Aladdin*'s technical brilliance had been matched at script level, it would have been a classic. As it is, it's brilliant entertainment, but unlike *Beauty and the Beast*, has no lasting resonance.

Jurassic Park: **So what can we tell you about this movie that you didn't already know? Well, for one thing Tyrannosaurus Rex, Triceratops and several of the other beasties that inhabit Richard Attenborough's titular, genetically engineered theme park actually lived during the Cretaceous rather than the Jurassic period, but we'd have to be a real bunch of boring old pedants to point that out. Similarly, it would be churlish to complain about Jeff Goldblum's auto-pilot portrayal of Jeff Goldblum, or director Spielberg's characteristically mawkish attitudes towards children, or Richard Attenborough's boring soliloquy about flea-circuses, because every time one of these starts to irritate you, there's a dramatic appearance by one of the film's real stars – those dinosaurs.**

Talk about state-of-the-art special effects: strutting saurians surround the stars in seamless stampede; T. Rex tears after a truck intent on trampling its inhabitants; the truly terrifying raptors stalk tiny tots in a darkened laboratory. It's difficult to think of anything you could conceivably add to this film to improve it.

The House of the Spirits: It's obvious we're talking epic here, a big budget movie with a cast that includes such heavyweights as Streep and Irons as well as Glenn Close and Winona Ryder. But it's also one of those movies that's so weighed down by plot and performances that it frequently seems like an ordeal to sit through it. Irons plays Esteban Trueba, a self-made patriarch who rules his dynasty with an iron fist. He banishes his spinster sister (Close) from his house when he thinks she is coming between him and his missus (Streep). And he tries to marry off his daughter (Ryder) to a wealthy European. But the headstrong Bianca is having a secret affair with a left-wing agitator, and, in the aftermath of a military coup, the diehard conservative Irons must decide whether his political loyalties are worth sacrificing his family for.

Based on a best-selling novel by Isabel Allende, this movie apparently took something like $70 million at the box office worldwide, but it's difficult to see the attraction apart from the star names involved. It's slow and uninvolving and doesn't really succeed in conjuring up a realistic portrait of those troubled times in South America. It would help if any of the characters were remotely likeable but they're not – Irons and Streep are a most unattractive screen pairing. Your spirits are likely to sink watching it.

Vocabulary: Films

1 On the sheet in your vocabulary notebook headed FILMS, note down all the words and expressions from these reviews which have a special association with films. For example, *opening line, portrayal, biggest grossing film* from the *Forrest Gump* review.

2 Write six sentences about the films or TV programmes you thought about at the beginning of the unit. Use as many of the words and expressions as possible from the FILMS section in your vocabulary notebook.

Grammar: Complex sentences

A complex sentence is one that consists of at least two clauses; in other words it has a main clause and at least one subordinate clause. Common types of subordinate clause are relative clauses and adverbial clauses (telling the reader more about time, reason or condition, for instance).

1 Look at the sentences below. Underline the subordinate clauses, then note whether they are examples of relative clauses or adverbial clauses.

a Aznavour is excellent as the bar room pianist who gets involved with gangsters.

b Irons plays Esteban Trueba, a self-made patriarch who rules his dynasty with an iron fist.

c He banishes his spinster sister (Close) from his house because he thinks she is coming between him and his missus (Streep).

d So what can we tell you about this movie that you didn't already know?

e Although Spielberg perhaps wasn't the best person to direct an adaptation of Alice Walker's novel about a poor black woman's life of hardship in the Deep South, he was probably one of the few directors with the clout to bring such material into the Hollywood mainstream.

f But it's also one of those movies that's so weighed down by plot and performances that it frequently seems like an ordeal to sit through it.

g If *Aladdin*'s technical brilliance had been matched at script level, it would have been a classic.

h Similarly, it would be churlish to complain about Jeff Goldblum's auto-pilot portrayal of Jeff Goldblum, or director Spielberg's characteristically mawkish attitudes towards children, or Richard Attenborough's boring soliloquy about flea-circuses, because every time one of these starts to irritate you, there's a dramatic appearance by one of the film's real stars – those dinosaurs.

i As it is, it's brilliant entertainment, which, unlike *Beauty and the Beast*, has no lasting resonance.

2 Complete these relative clauses on the topic of film in any way that you like.

a .... is a film which …

b .... is an actor who …

c In the local cinema at the moment is a film called ...., which …

d I really liked the scene in .... where …

e The most memorable moment I've ever seen on celluloid was the one when …

3 Complete these adverbial clauses on the topic of film in any appropriate way.

a I enjoyed the film .... because …
b I would have enjoyed the film .... much more if …
c Although .... is a very famous actor, …
d The film .... is at its most successful when …
e The film .... was a great box office success since …

4 Compare the sentences you wrote in Exercises 2 and 3 with those written by other students.

5 Many complex sentences involve having a verb in the form of a present or past participle in the subordinate clause. For example:

Based *on a best-selling novel by Isabel Allende, this movie apparently took something like $70 million at the box office worldwide.*
or:
*Now **showing** in British cinemas, Forrest Gump is unlikely to be as successful here as it was in the States.*

Answer these questions.

a If the sentences in the examples were each written as a couple of simple sentences rather than one long complex one, what would those simple sentences be?
b Why does the first example use the past participle *based*, whereas the second example uses the present participle *showing*?

6 Look at the sentences below about films. In each case a present or past participle is needed to complete the sentence. Choose the appropriate verb from the box below, put it into a suitable participle form and complete the sentences.

> seat populate act shoot cover
> send set cash regard draw

a .... at a Georgia bus stop, Forrest Gump (Hanks) relates his remarkable life story in a slow southern drawl, ... everything from his 1950s childhood to his involvement in many of the most important events of the next three decades.

b .... upon African sounds and rhythms, Hans Zimmer's outstanding score makes up for the syrupy lyrics and lack-lustre tunes.
c .... in a world .... exclusively by animals and untouched by human hand, *The Lion King* is a bold and impressive achievement.
d Highly .... as a drama, *Tokyo Story* tells of two elderly parents who visit their married children for the first time only to find they're an inconvenience.
e Evocatively .... on location in war-torn Vienna, *The Third Man* tells the story of writer Holly Martins, who arrives in the city to join his chum, Harry Lime, only to learn that he has been killed in an accident. Or has he?
f Amusingly .... up the role that made her famous in *The Exorcist*, Linda Blair is let down in *Repossessed* by lame material and slack direction.
g .... in his premium bonds, Hancock relocates to Paris's Left Bank where his naive paintings and half-baked philosophy initially attract little attention.
h Superbly ...., this adaptation of Stan Barstow's novel, *A Kind of Loving*, is about a northern draughtsman forced into an unhappy marriage.

7 Look back at the sentences you wrote in Vocabulary Exercise 2. Re-work those sentences to make them into complex sentences. If you prefer, write new sentences from scratch. Write at least one sentence with a relative clause, one with an adverbial clause of some kind, one beginning with a present participle and one beginning with a past participle. Compare your sentences with those written by other students.

Speaking: Criticising tactfully

The film didn't hold my attention all the time.

English people often do not like to express criticism directly. The reviewer of *Forrest Gump*, for instance, if asked by the producer what he thought of the film would find it hard to say 'I found it boring' or 'It was far too long'. He would be much more likely to express his feelings in a slightly less direct way. He might say, for example, 'I didn't find it terribly interesting' or 'It was a bit lengthy' or 'I think it might have been improved by being somewhat shorter'.

The methods used in the examples in the previous paragraph are:

a giving the negative of the opposite of one's opinion; to say 'That's not true' sounds much gentler than 'That's a lie'. Similarly, 'She is unsuccessful' sounds less severe than 'She is a failure'.

b using an understatement; if a teacher says 'Your son's work is a little careless', then the boy's parents will be much less upset than if the teacher says 'Your son's work is a mess' and 'the storyline's rather weak' is much less potentially upsetting than 'the storyline's weak'.

c making the statement sound personal rather than an absolute truth by using expressions like 'I think' or 'in my opinion'.

d using modals of possibility, like *might, may* or *could* also make the opinion sound much less firm and definite.

1 📼 Listen to the situations on the tape. Respond politely and tactfully, using the methods suggested above.

2 Rewrite Pat's answers using the methods outlined above in order to make the criticisms less potentially hurtful to Chris.

CHRIS: Did you enjoy the weekend you spent at my sister's?

PAT: It was terrible. It rained all the time. There was nothing to do there and your sister's cooking is disgusting.

CHRIS: What did you do on Saturday evening?

PAT: We went to a film. It was dreadful. The actors were appalling, the story was one long cliché and the camerawork was dull.

CHRIS: What about Sunday?

PAT: We went for a walk along the river but it was freezing and we couldn't wait to get back home. When we did, the electricity wasn't working – your sister must have forgotten to pay the bill – so we couldn't use the heating or the cooker. I went to bed to try to get some warmth back into my body. But the bed was so lumpy and uncomfortable that I got up after half an hour and decided to catch the earliest possible bus home.

CHRIS: When are you going to see her again?

PAT: Not for a long time, I hope.

3 📼 Remember that intonation is very important in conveying the speaker's mood. A flat intonation can sound aggressive whereas a fall-rise sounds polite and friendly. Practise this by repeating the criticisms you hear on the tape.

4  Follow these instructions.

1 Listen to one version of the rewritten dialogue from Exercise 2 read with a flat intonation.
2 Now listen to it read with more fall-rise intonation patterns.
3 Practise both dialogues speaking at the same time as Pat on the tape.

5 Follow these instructions.

1 Work with your partner reading the dialogue in the way that you rewrote it. Take it in turns to be Pat. Both of you should read the dialogue first with an aggressive intonation and then in a polite and friendly way.
2 In the first reading, sound as angry as you like about the whole weekend. You will probably use a narrow vocal range to convey this mood.
3 In your second reading, you should sound as polite and friendly as you can. Your criticisms should sound quite light-hearted and jokey. You will need to use a lot of fall-rise intonation patterns to convey this mood.

6 Follow these instructions.

1 In pairs take one of the role play cards from your teacher. Think about how to do what the card says.
2 Perform the role play in front of the other students.
3 Comment on each other's performance.

Study skills: What to read in English

1 Watching films can be a very pleasant way of improving your English. You can, of course, also improve your English enormously by reading for pleasure in English. Discuss whether the statements below are true or false and then compare your answers with those that the teacher gives you.

a To learn as much as possible you should look up every word and expression that you don't understand.
b Reading English for pleasure helps you learn vocabulary.
c It is a mistake to waste time reading something that is really too easy for you.
d It is better to read a classic of culture than a piece of popular fiction.
e To get maximum benefit from any reading that you do, you should keep a notebook in which you write a quick summary of and comments on any book you read.
f It is better to read for fifteen minutes every day than for two hours once a week.
g Ideally, you should always have a dictionary beside you as you read.
h You should be careful not to waste time on reading books that have examples of bad grammar or slang in them.

2 Which of the following have you ever read in English?

- the English version of something you've already read in your own language (it doesn't matter, of course, whether the original was in your language or English)
- the book of a film you've seen
- a newspaper or magazine
- something connected with your work or special area of study
- a cartoon book
- something that your school made you read
- a well-known book in English
- a library book
- something recommended by a friend

3 What was your opinion of what you read? Would you recommend what you have read? Why (not)?

4 Which English-speaking writers have you heard of? Can you name any books by them? Do you know what kinds of books they wrote, e.g. crime stories, thrillers, romance, historical novels, humour, short stories, etc.?

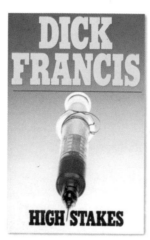

Have you read anything by these writers in English? Have you read any books by any of them in translation? If so, do you think you might enjoy reading them in English? Why (not)?

The main
aspects of
language
worked on in
this unit are:
- listening to lectures
- pronunciation of consonant groups
- continuous verb forms
- word associations

Warm-up: Women's language

You are going to listen to part of a lecture entitled *Verbal Hygiene for Women: Linguistics Misapplied*.

What do you think the lecture might be about?

Reading: Language and women's place

1 The lecturer, a linguist called Deborah Cameron, refers to the work of Robin Lakoff who has written on the subject of gender differences between men's and women's use of language. First read an extract from *Language and Women's Place*, a book by Lakoff which Cameron refers to.

In this book, Lakoff argues that women use a different kind of language than men do. Compared with men, women use:

- fewer taboo words
- more question tags
- some vocabulary which men would rarely if ever use (*mauve, divine, adorable,* etc.)
- more tentative language (*might be* rather than *is*, for example)
- requests rather than orders when asking someone to do something (*Won't you close the door* rather than *Close the door*).

In this extract, Lakoff is commenting on the effect which using a different kind of language has on women's place in society.

Read the extract and answer the questions that follow it.

> It will be found that the overall effect of 'women's language' … is that it submerges a woman's personal identity, by denying her the means of expressing herself strongly, on the one hand, and encouraging expressions that suggest triviality in subject matter and uncertainty about it… Of course, other forms of behaviour in this society have the same purpose, but the phenomenon seems especially clear linguistically.
>
> The ultimate effect of these discrepancies is that women are systematically denied access to power, on the grounds that they are not capable of holding it as demonstrated by their linguistic behaviour along with other aspects of their behaviour.

a Which of the characteristics of women's language suggest that a woman is denied 'the means of expressing herself strongly'?

b Which of the characteristics of women's language suggest triviality in subject matter and uncertainty about it?

c Do you think that there are similar differences between men and women's use of language in your own society?

d Have you had any experiences of men or women's use of language which would either support or contradict Lakoff's argument?

e If Lakoff's arguments are correct, what do you think could be done, from a language point of view, to help women have easier access to positions of power in society?

2 Look at this advertisement for a course. What sorts of things do you think the tutors might do or say on a course like this? Do you think such courses would be effective? Would you like to attend one? Why or why not?

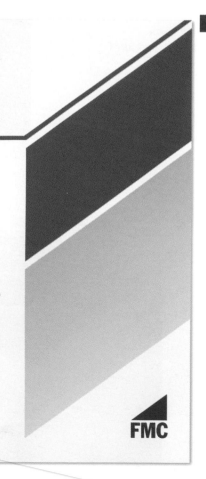

Assertiveness for Women

One-day Seminar

- *Would you like to be more successful?*
- *Are there men in your company who earn more than you although they are less able?*
- *Do you ever find it difficult to say exactly what you mean?*
- *Do you ever feel that being a woman is a disadvantage in your career?*
- *Do you ever say yes when you would rather say no?*

Many women do not achieve the success they deserve because they are not assertive enough. Women do not speak or behave as assertively as men do and so they are not as successful as men are.

Attend our seminar and our highly trained and widely experienced lecturers will show you how to be more assertive. For just £200 you can learn how to assert your right to succeed.

FMC

Listening: A lecture

1 In her lecture, Deborah Cameron is particularly concerned by the way expensive short courses are organised and women's magazine articles are written with the aim of changing the way women speak. She has just quoted from one such magazine article which criticised women for being too hesitant and tentative in their speech.

🔊 Listen to the first part of the extract from the lecture and complete these skeleton notes.

Source of mag. article = Robin Lakoff,
19   ,
In this bk. RL describes a distinctive
register in English'   ,
(Opposite =   )
This register characterised by:
 1 hedge words (perhaps etc.)
 2
 3
 4 polite expressions
Women use such lang. because

Result of using such lang. =

The argument in this bk. has resulted in

2 🔊 Now listen to the second part of the extract and take your own notes on what you hear. Use any style of note-taking that you prefer. Remember how abbreviations, numbered points, initials, drawings and punctuation can all help you to write quick and clear notes (see Unit 16).

Compare your notes with those written by a partner. Do your partner's notes make you want to add anything to your own or change anything in your own?

3 🔊 Listen again to the lecture and decide whether the following statements about it are true or false.

a Deborah Cameron thinks highly of Robin Lakoff's book.
b Lakoff claims that women's language is more tentative and much less certain than neutral language.
c Lakoff claims that women's language is an obstacle to their professional progress.
d Organisers of courses to improve women's language have misinterpreted Lakoff's work.
e Lakoff's findings are supported by a lot of facts and figures.
f According to Cameron, there are no real differences in speech style between men and women.
g Cameron claims that what Lakoff terms women's language is really the language of people of either sex in subordinate positions.
h Cameron feels that training women in different speech styles has some potentially positive uses.

4 🔊 Listen again to the first part of the lecture and write it down as dictation.

Vocabulary: Word associations

1 🔊 Listen to the extract from the lecture again as you read the transcript on page 171. Underline any phrases which you think might typically be used in lectures, whatever their specific subject matter may be. In the first paragraph, for example, you might choose to underline such phrases as *scholarly research, the source of the article, published under the title, an influential book, a new line of enquiry.*

2 Write sentences using some of these words and expressions about your own special subject or an area that you are particularly interested in.

3 In the table below there are some words from the lecture. Using a dictionary, if necessary, complete the table. Note that it may not be possible to fill in all the blanks, but it may be possible to put more than one word in some of the blanks.

Noun	Verb	Adjective	Adverb
authority		influential distinctive charming competent	
communicator exception generalisation	provide		
theorist		intervening	
assessment		different	
		negative	

4 Now use words from the table to complete the sentences.

a As a Glaswegian, I had to take .... to the rude remarks he made about the Scots.

b Jill has a very good .... understanding of pedagogy but not very much practical experience.

c A lot of students' marks nowadays depend on continuous .... rather than on end-of-term examinations.

d Although the twins look identical, their characters .... significantly.

e The twins are identical. Even their own mother sometimes finds it hard to .... Rowena from Rosanna.

f German Romantic poets had a very strong .... on the poetry of Lord Byron.

g Manuel's use of English isn't very accurate, but he's still very good at .... what he wants to say.

h I hate it when people make sweeping .... – saying things, for example, like 'women are less good at maths than men'.

i She has such an attractive personality that I think she could .... the most miserable of misogynists.

j We haven't seen each other since we were at school together and an awful lot has happened in the .... years.

Speaking: Pronunciation of consonant groups

1 Some words in English can be difficult to pronounce because they have two or three consonants pronounced together without a vowel sound between them e.g. *scholarly, professional, complicated, competent*. Look at the transcript of the lecture on pages 171–2 and find six more examples of words with two or more consonant sounds pronounced together (in any position in the word).

2 ▭ Say these words after the speaker on the tape.

> please still sings scratch black
> skin loved clothes prize smell
> laughs depths twice slow laughter
> triumphs through tipped myths
> twelfth spill baked splendid bulbs

3 ▭ Repeat the sentences which you hear after the speaker on the tape.

4 Can you think of at least two words which have each of these consonant sounds together unseparated by a vowel sound?

/br/ /ps/ /lth/ /bd/ /ʃr/ /str/

Work with a partner. Take it in turns to say the words you thought of to a partner. Your partner should try to write down the words you say.

5 Write sentences using as many of the words practised in Exercises 1–4 as possible.

Practise saying the sentences you have written.

Grammar: Continuous forms

1 Complete this sentence.

Continuous verb forms always consist of the verb, *to*
.... + ...

2 Look again at the tapescript for the lecture extract on pages 171–2 and underline all the examples of continuous forms of a verb. Now answer these questions.

  a Why are continuous forms of the verb used in each of these instances?
  b Would it have been possible to use a simple form of the verb in the same place? If so, how would this have affected the meaning of what was being said?
  c Why, do you think, are simple verb forms used much more by Deborah Cameron in her lecture?

3 Complete the table.

Continuous forms of the verb to do

Tense	Form
past perfect	had been doing
	was/were doing
present perfect	
	am/is/are doing
future	
	will/shall have been doing
conditional	
	would have been doing
infinitive	
might	
	must be doing
should have	
	ought to have been doing

4 Look at the pairs of sentences below. What is the difference in meaning between the simple and the continuous form of the verb in each case?

1 a Bill had learnt Japanese before he went to live in Tokyo.
1 b Nicky had been learning Japanese before she went to live in Tokyo.
2 a Sue left the house when her brother arrived.
2 b Anna was leaving the house when her brother arrived.
3 a I've drunk six cups of coffee this morning.
3 b I've been drinking coffee all morning.
4 a Joan lives in New York.
4 b Jean is living in New York.
5 a What are you doing?
5 b What do you do?

6 a Tomorrow afternoon Danny will be lying on a beach in Spain.
6 b Tomorrow afternoon Norma will meet the children from school.
7 a By this time next year I'll have worked for this company for ten years.
7 b By this time next year I'll have been working for this company for ten years.
8 a I would make more of an effort to help if I were you.
8 b I would be making more of an effort to help if I were you.
9 a I'd love to be going on holiday with you.
9 b I'd love to go on holiday with you.
10 a Matthew might have written the poem.
10 b Mark might have been writing a poem.

5 These verbs are rarely found in the continuous form:

admire appear be believe
belong to consist of contain desire
despise detest dislike envy exist
forget fit hate have hear
imagine know lack last like
love look like mean own
possess prefer matter recognise
remember see seem sound
suppose suspect understand want
wish

Divide these verbs into categories under the headings:

(Dis)liking Ownership The mind
Nature of being Sight and hearing

Note: there is not one right way of categorising these verbs. Do it in the way that seems most logical to you.

Can you suggest a reason why they are not often used in the continuous?

6 When the verbs above are used in the continuous form, then they tend to have a distinct meaning. What exactly does the verb in italics mean in the sentences below?

a The judge *will be hearing* the case some time next week.

b *I've been meaning* to ring you for ages.
c *I am seeing* the boss at 2.30 tomorrow.
d My favourite actress *is appearing* in a play at the Lyric this week.

e Her little boy's *being* rather naughty at the moment.
f We *were having* dinner when Jack burst into the room.
g Molly *is having* a party next week.
h Janet's *having* a baby next month.
i John *was having* a bath when the phone rang.

7 Discuss with a partner whether you feel these statements are true or false.

a Continuous forms of the verb are referred to as progressive forms in some grammar books.
b The present continuous infinitive form is *to be done*.
c The present continuous passive form is *am/is/are being done*.
d Continuous forms of the verb often focus on the situation at one particular point of time – past, present or future.
e Continuous forms of the verb are often used to emphasise that an action takes some time to complete.
f Past continuous forms are often used to list the different events in a story.
g Present continuous forms are often used to describe things that happen repeatedly.
h There is no future continuous form of some verbs, e.g. *to have*.

8 Now choose the most probable form of the verb for these sentences.

a The actors *live / are living* with Italian families while the Italian scenes of the film *are / are being* shot. Today they *film / are filming* a fight in the central square of the town and this area *has been closed / has been being closed* to traffic for the whole day. Films *are often made / are often being made* in this town because it *has altered / has been altering* so little since medieval times.
b As she *closed / was closing* the door of the house, Polly *noticed / was noticing* how the sun *shone / was shining* and the birds *sang / were singing* and she *began / was beginning* to feel happier than she *had felt / had been feeling* for a long time.
c Ricky *will soon start / will soon be starting* work at his father's restaurant. He *will work / will be working* there for six months until he *goes / is going* to university. At the moment he *plans / is planning* to study business administration at university but I *think / am thinking* that he *may decide / may be deciding* to change to economics and politics.

The main aspects of language worked on in this unit are:
- reading scientific articles
- expressing concepts in science
- tautologies
- summarising
- checking your reading speed

Warm-up: Scientific experiments

Discuss the following with a partner.

a Have you ever taken part in a psychological experiment? If so, what did you have to do and what was its aim?

b Twins can be useful in psychology experiments in one area in particular. What do you think the area might be and why would twins be useful?

c Do you know any twins? Are they identical or fraternal? How similar are they in terms of character and tastes?

Reading: A scientific article

A scientific article is usually characterised by a number of features – its organisation, its vocabulary, its precision and its structures. Read the article on the next two pages and then do the exercises below on these aspects of scientific writing.

1 The six paragraphs in the article on the next two pages could be given the headings below but not in this order. Write the number of the paragraph beside its heading.

- ☐ Aims/rationale of experiment
- ☐ Comments
- ☐ Conclusions
- ☐ Description of experiment
- ☐ Explanation of conclusions
- ☐ Introduction

2 Work in pairs and answer these questions.

a What were the aims of the experiment?
b How was it set up?
c What conclusions were drawn?
d What explanation is provided for the results?

3 Read the article again and underline all the words and expressions which you think you would frequently find in scientific writing, e.g. *psychologists, defined.*

Which of these categories does each of your underlined words and expressions belong to?

a Those (e.g. *psychologist*) with a close association with a particular field of science.
b Those (e.g. *defined*) which are important for scientific writing in general.

4 It is, by definition, important that scientific writing should be precise; it must state clearly exactly what happened. This is done by:

a using specific vocabulary (*round metal container* or *shallow 3cm. dish* rather than just *container* or *dish,* for example);

b stating exact numbers and percentages;

c providing pertinent factual information about what happened;

d suggesting reasons;

e making tentative claims like '*X concluded that* fat people are happier' or '*their results suggest that* fat people are happier' rather than making an unqualified statement such as 'fat people are happier'.

Find examples of all these five ways of writing precisely in the article, *Love is blind … to genes.*

5 *Love is blind … to genes* is an article from *New Scientist*, the main British magazine for those interested in science. It is, however, intended to have a reasonably broad appeal and so there are some features of popular journalism in the writing as well. Can you find any examples of this, i.e. features of the writing that you would not find in a straight scientific report aimed solely at behaviour geneticists?

Love is blind … to genes

Rosie Mestel, Los Angeles

HOW DO I love thee? Psychologists have been counting the ways for decades, and have defined styles of romance that range from wild and passionate to cosy and affectionate. Now psychologists in California have published the first ever twin study on the subject. Genes, they found, have little to do with a person's attitudes to love. The result is a surprise, given the wealth of genetic studies on personality traits such as introversion-extroversion, aggression and even leisure-time activities, many of which are strongly influenced by genes. Such studies generally compare identical twins – whose genes are the same – with fraternal twins, who have roughly half their genes in common. If a trait is influenced by genes, identical twins should be more similar to each other than fraternal twins are. If genes are irrelevant, identical twins should be no more similar than fraternal twins.

Niels Waller and Philip Shaver, psychologists at the University of California at Davis, undertook the first ever genetic study of love attitudes 'in part because everybody's interested in the topic', says Waller, but also because they are studying the larger issue of how people make emotional attachments to each other.

Waller and Shaver recruited 445 pairs of twins, three-quarters of them identical and a quarter fraternal. A quarter of the pairs were male, three-quarters female. Each twin filled in a questionnaire designed to identify six basic love styles

described by sociologist John Lee of the University of Toronto. These are Eros, Ludus, Storge, Pragma, Mania and Agape. Roughly speaking, Eros is a wild and passionate lover, Ludus enjoys the fun of love but is unwilling to commit, Storge is companionable and dependable, Agape is selfless, Pragma is practical, Mania is jealous and unstable. The twins were instructed to note how strongly they agreed or disagreed with statements such as 'I try to keep my lover a little uncertain about my commitment to him/her', or 'Our love-making is very passionate and exciting'. As a control, the twins answered other questions designed to measure personality traits known to be influenced by genes. As expected, these elicited very similar types of answers from identical twins.

Of all six love styles, Waller and Shaver found that five had hardly any genetic influence; the answers from identical twins were almost as similar as those from fraternal twins. Only Mania stood out as influenced by genes, which Waller says is not surprising because other researchers have found that neurotic personalities are genetically influenced. For the other five love types,

environmental influences were paramount, although the study does not reveal what those factors are. The researchers found that spouses were very similar to their partners in love attitudes, more so than twins were to each other. The exception was for people with Mania and Ludus love attitudes. Perhaps, speculates Waller, two super-jealous partners or two 'free spirits' cannot sustain relationships easily.

Why should love be blind to genes? The answer is not clear; Waller says, 'It could be that parents don't try to influence the personality of their children that much.' That would mean basic personality is relatively unmoulded by parental influence, giving genes more sway. 'But what I've been finding in my studies is that parents do get involved in their children's mate choices.' If this is the case, choosing a mate would be much more directed by parents and less by genes.

'It's interesting and I find it surprising,' says David Rose, a behaviour geneticist at the University of Arizona. How about a reason? 'You can make up any nice romantic explanation you want for why it should be,' he says. 'But I don't have the answer.'

6 Discuss these questions in groups.

a Do you think people can be categorised according to their 'love type'?

b Can you suggest any statements that could have been used in the questionnaire to identify different love types?

c Can you suggest any explanation for the findings of the experiment?

d What do you think society gains, if anything, from experiments like this?

e Can you suggest any further experiments that could be done to deepen understanding in this area of behaviour psychology?

f In general, what is your reaction to the experiment described in this article?

Grammar: Expressing concepts in science

1 Scientific writing is characterised by a number of structures. What do you think those are? Answer the questions below and find an example for each from the *Love is blind … to genes* article.

a Which tense would scientists use when describing things that are always true?

b Which verb form is particularly useful when scientists want to focus on *what* is done rather than on *who* is doing it?

c Which verb forms are particularly useful when the scientist is discussing his or her conclusions and wants to make it clear that the explanations suggested are not yet established as fact?

d Which structures are particularly useful when scientists want to talk about what happens or would happen under various conditions?

2 Here are some sentences from a scientific text where some of the verb forms have been altered. Underline the verb forms which you think are not the original ones and replace them with something that is more typical of standard scientific writing. You may need to make other changes to the sentences as well.

a The aim of the experiment was to establish whether only children are doing better in their later professional lives.

b Three psychologists analysed the career patterns of two hundred only children and two hundred people with one or more siblings and then they compared them using standard statistical methods.

c The results possibly show that there is perhaps a small correlation between being an only child and later career success.

d The results show that if a boy is an only child, it will be more of a career advantage for him than it will be for a girl.

e Suppose the scientists could take all other factors fully into account, however, they will be sure to find that some of those other factors are of far greater importance than whether a person is an only child or not.

3 ⌨ Listen to the tape and then write sentences about the experiment which you hear being described. Write sentences using the following forms in any appropriate way.

a the present simple
b the passive
c *may* or *might*
d zero conditional
e second conditional

4 If possible, find an article relating to a branch of science which is of particular interest to you personally. Answer these questions.

a To what extent do the paragraph headings listed in Reading Exercise 1 also apply to your article?

b Answer Reading Exercises 2 and 3 on page 143 with regard to your own article.

c Are there examples of the structures discussed in the previous exercise in your own article?

d Do you notice anything else interesting about the structures used in your own article?

Tell other students about some of the things you learnt (both about language and about science) from looking at your own article.

Vocabulary: Tautologies

1 In the paragraph below there are twelve examples of tautologies which are common in English today. Read the passage and decide what tautology is.

2 Shorten the paragraph by removing all the unnecessary words.

> We employed a business consultant to give us some advice on our company's future plans. He told us that it was an absolute certainty that the end result of handing out free gifts to each and every one of our customers would be an increase in sales. We should also gain the added bonus of enhancing customer loyalty to the company as they would find our approach quite distinct from that of our competitors. He concluded by saying that it was the honest truth that all our financial problems would be past history if we took on board the forward planning proposals he was recommending. He insisted that his recommendations were absolutely perfect for our situation and that we would never want to revert back to our old way of doing business.

Writing: Summaries

Writing a summary means writing an outline of a text using far fewer words. This means cutting out anything in the original text that is not essential and expressing the main ideas of the original as concisely as you can.

1 The first paragraph of the article in the *Love is blind … to genes* text can be summarised in the following way. There are, of course, many other possible ways to summarise it.

Californian psychologists have investigated the extent to which twins' love styles differ. They have compared identical to fraternal twins to determine the effect which genes have on love style. If genes are important then the love styles of identical twins should be closer than those of fraternal twins, as they are for traits like extroversion-introversion, leisure tastes, etc. (59 words)

The original first paragraph of the text is 144 words long.

Answer these questions.

a Why does the summary ignore the first two sentences of the original?
b Why does the summary not mention the conclusion in the first paragraph as the original does?
c How does the summary deal with the last two sentences of the original?
d What other extra details from the original text have been omitted from the summary?

2 Tick the points from an original text which should be retained in a summary and put a cross against those which would normally be dropped when writing a summary.

full explanations
examples
the main points of the text
analogies
names
background information
definitions
tautological expressions (e.g. *a brave and courageous man*)
comments
descriptions of people

3 The rest of the original *Love is blind … to genes* article is 570 words in length. Complete the summary of it using about 140 words.

Study skills: Checking your reading speed

1 In Unit 8, you worked out your reading speed and read about a technique for improving it. Has your reading speed in English increased since then?

Read the text below for one minute and count the number of words you have read. Compare the number with what you wrote down at the end of Unit 8.

JUST WATCH THE
EYES

When we are challenged to think about something, we usually look slightly upward and either to the right or to the left. Merle E. Day, a psychologist at the Downey Illinois Veterans Administration Hospital, reported in 1964 that each of us can be classified as a left-mover or a right-mover, in that each person tends to turn their eyes in the same direction about 75 percent of the time. (Women are less consistent than men in this regard.) The numbers of right-movers and left-movers are about equal in any large group.

Day then discovered that the direction of the eye-turn appears to be a marker of a wide variety of psychological and physiological characteristics. Left-movers and right-movers differ in their degree of attention, use of language, brain-wave patterns, muscle tone and response to psychotherapy.

A left-mover, according to Day, tends to have a heightened awareness of subjective, internal experiences. More recently Paul Bakan of Simon Fraser University found that left-movers are significantly more susceptible to hypnosis than right-movers, as measured by the Stanford Hypnotic Susceptibility Link, a standard test. Bakan has also found that left-movers score higher than right-movers in the Scholastic Aptitude Test, as well as showing greater fluency in writing, while right-movers tend to score higher in the mathematics portion. Bakan further reports that right-movers are more likely to twitch and have tics than left-movers, spend less time asleep (if they're males), prefer cool colors and make earlier choices of a career. Left-movers, on the other hand, tend to imagine more vividly, are more sociable, more likely to become alcoholic (if they're males) and are more likely to report themselves as musical and religious. To find out whether you are a right-mover or a left-mover may be troublesome, because the simple effort of trying to find out may cause a self-consciousness that may stand in the way of an answer. Perhaps all you can do is to start becoming aware of the direction in which you flick your eyes when you confront a problem or question. Determining a friend's tendency ought to be easier if the friend doesn't know what you're trying to find out. Just face her/him fairly straight-on and ask a few questions like the following:

1 How do you spell *perpendicular* (or for that matter *parallel*)?
2 What is the product of 11 by 15?
3 How would you define *virtue* or *sin* (or *mashed potatoes*)?

Ignore the answers. Just watch the eyes.

2 Finish reading the text and write a summary of it. The text is 410 words long; you should write about 140 words.

Killing a cad
Short story

The main aspects of language worked on in this unit are:	• listening to a short story • writing the beginning and ending of a story • the grammar of ellipsis • slang

Warm-up: Short stories

1 What are often features of a successful short story? Complete the list in the box below. You are given some of the letters in the missing words to help you – and the number of missing letters is indicated by the dashes.

- an intriguing op_ _ _ng paragraph
- interesting ch_ _ _ _ _ _rs
- evocative de_ _ _ _ _ _ _on of the setting
- hu_ _ur
- a strong p_ _t
- an unexpected e_ _ _ _g
- original use of la_ _ _ _ge
- effective use of di_ _ _ _ue
- l_ _e interest
- an ima_ _ _ _ _ _ve situation
- te_ _ _on
- a me_ _ _ge about, say, the nature of the human condition
- ....
- ....

2 Would you agree that all the characteristics listed in the box are in fact important for you in a short story?

Can you think of any other features that you would like to add to the box in the spaces provided?

3 Have you read any short stories recently (in any language)? If so, did they have any of the features listed in the box? Or can you think of any short stories you know which do have some of these features?

4 You are going to listen to a short story called *More than One Way to Kill a Cad*. Write down three things that the title makes you feel about the story.

For example: *I think the cad in the title might refer to someone's business partner who turned out to be dishonest.*

Compare your predictions with those written by other students.

Listening: *More than One Way to Kill a Cad*

1 🔊 Listen to the first part of the story *More than One Way to Kill a Cad* by Tony Steed.

2 🔊 Listen a second time and fill in as many as possible of the missing words in this passage.

She seemed such a (1) .... old dear. As I gulped down the last of her hot tea, I almost wished we were about to do something clean and (2) .... and decent. Like an armed raid on Dr Barnardo's. You see, she didn't really have (3) .... in her attic and never would have – not until me and Knuckles got up there, anyway. What she did have up there – according to the grapevine – was a (4) .... in ready cash … I emptied a handful of crumbs into an onyx (5) .... and motioned Knuckles to pick up the traps. Her (6) .... got the message and rose gracefully to her feet.

'It's a (7) .... climb to the top – such a (8) .... house,' she apologised. 'The upper part of the building is somewhat (9) .... I no longer employ (10) ....'

I (11) .... inwardly at this last bit of information and we followed the old girl up a succession of wide, marbled (12) .... On the top landing a (13) .... stretched up to the (14) .... Knuckles clambered up this and slid back the (15) .... steel bolts on the trap door.

Her ladyship smiled. 'Sir Percy, my (16) .... husband, was convinced that a (17) .... might be tempted to – ah – (18) .... in on us,' she explained. I nodded. One way and another Sir Percy seemed to have had a thing about burglars.

3 🔊 Listen to the second part of the story and answer the questions.

a What do the men think they are going to find in the attic?
b Why do they think it is there?
c What do they know about the old lady and her husband?
d What will they do if they find what they are looking for?

4 🔊 Listen to the third part of the story and answer the questions.

a What do the men find?
b What do they decide must have happened?
c What do you think the word *croaked* means in this context?
d What does Knuckles do when he realises what has happened?

5 ▣ Listen to the final part of the story and answer the questions.

   a What does the storyteller do after Knuckles leaves?
   b What is he planning to do next?
   c What is puzzling him?
   d What happens at the end of the story?
   e What do you think will happen next?

6 Work in pairs and discuss these questions.

   a Who is the cad in the story?
   b The narrator uses irony several times in the story. What is irony and what are the examples of it?
   c What is the connection between the first and the last paragraphs of the story?

7 ▣ Listen to the story again. This time read it at the same time (the tapescript is on pages 172–3) and prepare to discuss the following questions:

   a To what extent were the predictions you wrote in Warm-up Exercise 4 correct?
   b Which of the characteristics of a short story from the box on the first page of this unit is present in *More than One Way to Kill a Cad*?

Vocabulary: Slang

1 Choose five words or expressions from *More than One Way to Kill a Cad* that you would like to learn. Write them down:

   a in their context from the story
   b in a sentence of your own.

2 There are a lot of slang or very colloquial expressions in this story. Find the expressions listed below in the tapescript on pages 172–3 and try to guess from the context what they might mean. Then use a dictionary to check whether you guessed correctly.

   a have a thing about
   b funny old geezer
   c we grafted hard
   d phoned the law
   e that figures
   f he was giving her the run-around
   g she croaked him
   h you berk

3 Match the slang expressions in the left-hand column with their meanings in the right-hand column.

Straight up!	Don't be silly!
Leave it out!	He's in the pub.
He's a twit!	He's in prison.
What's the damage?	It's far too expensive!
He's rolling in it.	You can't fool me!
He's awesome.	He's very rich.
He's inside.	Honestly!
He's down the boozer.	He's fantastic.
Pull the other one!	How much is it?
What a rip-off!	He's a stupid person.

He's rolling in it!

4 Answer these questions.

   a Do you know any other slang expressions in English?
   b Why do people use slang?
   c Do you enjoy using slang in your own language and/or in English?
   d What sorts of words/concepts often have slang equivalents?
   e Why can it be risky for people who are not native-speakers to use slang?

5 Here are some slang expressions referring to some of those topics which have a particular wealth of slang expressions. Some of these words have 'normal' meanings as well as their slang ones. Write them down in the appropriate category for the slang meaning.

skint   banged up   the skunk   a wally
booze   gobsmacked   the fuzz   dosh
bread   to grass   a wimp   smashed

Money	Drink	People	Crime

6 Can you add any of the other slang expressions that you have discussed in this lesson to the columns in Exercise 5?

Grammar: Ellipsis

Ellipsis means leaving out words which are – or should be – obvious from the context. Sometimes, however, a speaker or writer's use of ellipsis can make it more difficult to follow what he or she is saying. There are quite a few examples in *More than One Way to Kill a Cad*. Indeed, the title itself is an example of ellipsis. (*There is* is not included in the title but it can be understood from the context.)

1 Here are some more sentences illustrating ellipsis from the story. What words have been missed out in these examples? (You will need to refer to the tapescript for a fuller context.)

a She didn't really have rats in her attic and never would have.
b Somewhere the late Sir Percy could gloat over his relics in privacy.
c Every chest, case and biscuit tin had to be pulled apart, every loose floorboard investigated.
d Somewhere nice and hospitable – like the Moon.
e Her ladyship knew he was giving her the run-around – and that's a pretty good motive.
f But he didn't.
g At the end of my fourth cigarette, I gave up.

2 Which words in the following sentences could be cut out (sometimes a word or two may have to be added to compensate) without affecting the meaning? Does it improve the style to cut these words out? If so, why?

a It seems ages since we've met or since we've even talked on the phone.
b Jane would always help you if she could help you.
c There are many people who know more about English grammar than I know about English grammar.
d The baby made a noise exactly like the kind of noise a kitten might make.
e Does he understand the problems you are going through?
No, he should understand them but he doesn't understand them.
f Women usually take some time off after having a baby whereas few men take any time off after their child is born.
g I'm afraid that I cannot help you and neither can anyone else help you.
h I would love to come to your party and Jack would like to come to it too.

Writing: Beginnings and endings

1 Here are the first sentences of four short stories. Are they effective? (i.e. do they make you want to read more?) Why or why not?

a The lives of most men are determined by their environment; they accept the circumstances amid which fate has thrown them not only with resignation but even with good will.
b The young man in the chocolate brown suit sat down at the table where the girl with the artificial camellia had been sitting for forty minutes.
c The room was warm and clean, the curtains drawn, the two table lamps alight – hers and the one by the empty chair opposite.
d The light was very bright when Margaret came out of the station.

2 Here are the final lines of the same four stories. Can you match the beginning sentence with the end sentence? What helped you to decide which sentences match?

i She walked on down the little lane between the blue painted tables.
ii And she walked out into the afternoon sunlight to collect all the shopping from the left-luggage, and go home to Harry.
iii He did what he wanted and he died when his goal was in sight and he never knew the bitterness of an end achieved.
iv And in the other room Mary Maloney began to giggle.

3 What do you think happened in each story? With a partner outline a plot to match one or more of the pairs of first and last lines. Compare your ideas with those of other pairs.

4 Your teacher will tell you what happened in the original stories. Did your stories coincide in any way with the originals?

5 With a partner compose the first sentence for a short story. Make up a sentence that would make you want to read on. Write the same sentence on two different pieces of paper. Give the pieces of paper to your teacher.

Now follow the further instructions which your teacher gives you.

The main aspects of language worked on in this unit are:

- reading drama
- speaking with a text
- expressing nuances of meaning through grammar
- adverbs of manner
- expressing feeling when you speak

Warm-up: Where people live

You are going to read the opening scene from *Benefactors*, a play by Michael Frayn, set in London in the mid-1980s. First look at the pictures.

Discuss these questions.

a What do you think might be the advantages and disadvantages of living in the terraced housing at the bottom?

b What do you think might be the advantages and disadvantages of living in the high-rise housing at the top?

c Have you experience of living in anything resembling either of these types of housing?

d Which do you think you would prefer to live in?

e When do you think that English roads called Basuto Road, Matabele Road and Mafeking Road would have been built?

f Are streets in your country ever named after historic events or places?

g Are they named after people, after flowers or trees, after geographical areas, after particular trades or occupations?

h Do some roads simply have numbers?

i What other types of road names are there in your country?

Reading: Benefactors

1 Each of the students in the class will read the part of one of the three characters in this scene – Jane, David or Colin. Sheila does not speak, but she is present for part of the scene and is the other main character of the play. Follow these instructions.

1 Silently read through the text, paying particular attention to your character. What do you learn about your character? What is his or her relationship to the other characters in the scene? What do you think his or her personality is like?

2 When you have read the scene and have thought about the questions above, get together with some other students who will be playing the same part and discuss your answers to the questions about your role.

3 As a class complete this box about the characters.

	Married to	Job	Personal characteristics
Jane			
David			
Colin			
Sheila			

4 If you were producing this play, what kind of set would you use for this first scene?

2 Before reading the text aloud, check that you understand it fully by answering the following comprehension questions.

a Jane is sometimes speaking now and sometimes her words are from the past. In the first part of the text, before David exits, all Jane's speeches are now, whereas David's are all from the past. What about Jane's speeches in the remainder of the extract?

b Why was Basuto Road to be pulled down? How did David feel about it? How did the people who lived there probably feel about the plans?

c There are quite a lot of words in the script which refer to aspects of light and darkness. What are they and what is their significance?

d In the extract there are hints in what Jane says about how things would change in the future. What are those hints and what do they suggest?

e What does Jane mean by what she says about kings and queens? What game is she referring to?

3 Underline any words in the text which you think the actors would give special emphasis to when speaking.

DAVID: Basuto Road! I love the name!

JANE: Basuto Road. How I hate those sour grey words!

DAVID: Basuto Road, SE15. And you can practically see it. Victorian South London. Two-storey terraces with tiny front gardens. You can practically smell the grey lace curtains in those bay windows. Don't you think?

JANE: You look back in life and there's a great chain of cloud-shadows moving over the earth behind you. All the sharp bright landscape you've just travelled through has gone grey and graceless.

DAVID: Basuto Road. But when you think how fresh and hopeful that must have sounded once, back in 1890! I suppose we'd just annexed Basutoland. East Africa was as new as outer space. The empire was as desirable as television. Bechuana Road and Matabele Road and Mashoma Road and Barotse Road.

JANE: Then ten years, fifteen years away behind you the land's out in sunlight again. You can see everything small and shining in the distance – so clear you feel you could reach out and touch it.

DAVID: Plus Maud Road, Daisy Road, Frances Road and Phoebe Road. I suppose they were the builder's daughters. Rather sad – it's all coming down. About fifteen acres. What do you think?

JANE: Basuto Road. It started in the sunlight. He was happy then. Yes! He was! He was happy! He came back in the middle of the day to tell me about the job, and he was like a child with a new bicycle. Ten years ago? No, twelve or more. But that day at any rate, that's out in the sunlight again.

DAVID: It's probably an impossible site. It's jammed between a railway line and a main road. What do you think?

JANE: He couldn't sit still. He couldn't stop talking about it.

DAVID: It's zoned at 150 to the acre. I bet it's more like 200. I'll need you to check that for me.

JANE: We were both still children. Middle-aged children.

DAVID: It would be a huge job. But that's where the work is. In local authority housing. That's where the real architecture's being done. So what do you think?

JANE: What did I think? I don't know. I can't remember. I expect I was against it. I expect I raised all kinds of sensible objections. That's the way we operated then. David was for things. I was against them. Government and Opposition. And we'd always settle the question democratically. One for, one against – motion carried.

DAVID: I'll go and have a quick look at the site. Ring Bill, oh, and Geoffrey Lewis. Tell them I've been called away.

Exit David

JANE: And that was fair because when I voted against, I was really voting for. In those days. Anything David was for, I was for. I wasn't going to tell *him* that, of course. Anyway, I had to come out in favour of the project soon enough because Colin was against it.

Enter Colin

JANE: David was for it, so Colin was against it. Colin was against it, so I had to be for it.

COLIN: I gather David's landed one of those great slum clearance jobs. Changing the face of London. So he's on his way up in the world.

JANE: Not that Colin cared much. Not then. He was mildly sardonic. But then he always was.

COLIN: What do you think about it, Jane?

JANE: King against king. Queen on her colour.

COLIN: I said what do you think about it.

JANE: A twilight area.

COLIN: A twilight area?

JANE: Not a slum clearance scheme, Colin. Not a slum.

COLIN: A twilight area. It sounds very beautiful.

Enter Sheila and David left.

JANE: Isn't that right, David?

DAVID: What's that, my love?

JANE: Basuto Road – a twilight area?

DAVID: It's certainly not a slum, whatever a slum is. No worse than this neighbourhood really. Or no worse than it used to be. A bit grey and exhausted that's all.

COLIN: It's got to be cleared, though. Otherwise those areas where the architects and demolition contractors live will start to look grey and exhausted again.

DAVID: I don't know why I put up with you, Colin. Everyone else takes me seriously.

COLIN: I take you seriously, David. You're building the bright new world we're all going to be living in.

DAVID: You sit at my table eating my food and drinking my wine … where's your glass?

COLIN: Sheila takes you seriously, anyway. She thinks the future's right there inside your head, like a chick about to burst out of an egg. Though she might feel rather at home in a sunset area.

JANE: A twilight area.

COLIN: Wouldn't you, my love?

DAVID: And don't start on Sheila again, for God's sake.

COLIN: You're going to be working on this one, are you, Jane? Down there with the clipboard? Doing market research?

JANE: I don't do market research.

COLIN: Good morning, madam. Would you like your house pulled down?

DAVID: They're going to get them pulled down whether they like it or not. And we don't need to ask them what they want instead because we know.

COLIN: Nice little semis with nice little gardens.

DAVID: The best popular housing to be devised.

COLIN: But you're not going to build them nice little semis with nice little gardens.

DAVID: I can't. I've got to show a net housing gain, not a colossal housing loss. What do you get with semis?

COLIN: Aesthetic typhoid, I expect.

DAVID: You get about thirty persons to the acre. I've got to house something more like 200. I'd have to cover the site with one solid fused mass of semi-detached housing.

COLIN: Sheila thinks that sounds wonderful.

JANE: Over dinner this would be. The children out of the way. Occasional clicks and whimpers on the baby-alarm from their two across the street. Colin and Sheila – I don't know – they seemed to live round here. She'd leave the

children here at some point in the day. That's what usually happened. Then when she came to collect them, she'd sit down for a cup of coffee and sooner or later she'd be saying, 'This is awful, I haven't done anything about the children's tea.' And I'd say, 'That's all right – they can have something here.' And then next thing I knew it would be, 'This is terrible, I haven't done anything about getting a meal for Colin.' And I'd say, 'Give him a ring – we've got plenty.' And she'd say, 'This is awful – we seem to live round here.' … No, we liked them. We really did. I wasn't just running a soup kitchen. Well, we liked them. David liked him. But he did actually urge David to build tower blocks! Quite funny when you think what happened later. It was just part of the game, of course. David was against them, so Colin was for them. He wasn't serious. David pretended not to be serious but in fact he was. That's why Colin could always get a rise out of him. Colin one end of the table, grinning. David the other end, frowning. Me putting in a word here and a word there, trying to redress the balance. And Sheila sitting there like the Dormouse not saying anything at all.

4 In groups of three, read through the extract from the play with as much feeling as you can.

5 Reading is one of the best ways to help you improve your feeling for collocations in English. In the sentences below some words are missing. Without referring to the text, can you remember what the word is? The initial letter is provided to help you.

a Jane would always r............................ objections.
b David was going to do some work for the local a............................
c Twelve votes for, ten a............................ – motion c............................
d David was changing the f............................ of London.
e David got involved in a slum c............................ scheme.
f He never seemed to take anything s............................, even if it was very important for everyone else.
g I've got to show a n............................ gain not a colossal l............................
h Jane would put in a w............................ here and there.

6 What do you think are the main differences between spoken and written English? Are the following characteristics most typical of written or of spoken English? Write W for written or S for spoken beside each characteristic.

Long complex sentences
Short simple sentences
Exclamations
Carefully structured paragraphs
Colloquial vocabulary
Repetitions
Meaning conveyed by stress and intonation
Meaning conveyed by punctuation
Contractions
Full verb forms
Ellipsis
Slang
False starts
Phrasal verbs
Strict adherence to rules of grammar and sentence structure
Rephrasing
Loose sentence structure
Unusual metaphors
Idioms

7 Drama is, of course, a kind of mixture of written and spoken English. The way characters speak is, in general, much more polished and controlled than the way people speak in everyday life. Yet good dialogue in modern plays certainly conveys the feel of spoken rather than written language. To what extent does the extract you have looked at from the play, *Benefactors*, sound like spoken rather than written English?

8 Imagine that Jane was writing a paragraph for her autobiography about the situation she was describing in the long speech at the end of the extract. Write the paragraph. Convey the points that she is making in her lines from the play but write in language appropriate to a book rather than a piece of drama. Begin:

It used to happen over dinner when the children were already in bed …

9 Discuss in pairs what you think will happen in the rest of the play.

Compare your ideas with those of other students in the class.

Study skills: Speaking with a text

In Unit 9, you practised speaking at the same time as a recorded cassette. It is particularly useful perhaps to do this with an example of spoken English.

1 ▭ Listen to a recording of Jane's last long speech at the end of the extract above. In your script mark the points where the actor takes a breath.

Stop the tape at each pause and repeat what has just been said. Remember to avoid giving too much importance to the 'weak' or unstressed syllables.

2 ▭ Play the tape again, speaking with Jane. Practise until you can keep up with the tape perfectly. Copy the actor's intonation as closely as you can.

3 Try reading the text again without the tape, using the same patterns of intonation as far as possible. If possible record yourself as you speak.

Grammar: Expressing nuances of meaning through grammar

Often grammar is a matter of choices. The structure you choose depends on the impression you mean to convey. Jane could have said *She left the children here at some point in the day*. Instead she chose to say, *She'd leave the children here at some point in the day. She'd leave* instead of the simple past emphasises the fact that Sheila habitually behaved in this way.

1 Underline all the other examples of *would* used to emphasise habit in Jane's last long speech in the extract from the play.

2 Follow these instructions.

1 Write a paragraph about yourself as a young child using *would* to convey the idea of habit at least three times.
2 Read out another student's paragraph. The rest of the class must try to guess who the writer of the paragraph was.

3 Compare the difference in nuance between the sentences in the pairs below. Note that all the sentences are perfectly correct and could be used in identical contexts but the grammatical differences between them allow the speakers to convey subtle nuances of implication or tone.

Remember that intonation is also important in conveying nuances of meaning.

1 a I wonder if you could help me.
1 b I was wondering if you could help me.
2 a I'll be surprised if I pass my driving test.
2 b I'd be surprised if I passed my driving test.
3 a I may come to the party this evening.
3 b I might come to the party this evening.
4 a Jim always calls me late at night.
4 b Jim's always calling me late at night.
5 a We heard the postman knock on the door.
5 b We heard the postman knocking on the door.
6 a Sheila'll do what Jane asks her to do.
6 b Sheila'll do whatever Jane asks her to do.
7 a Help me carry the trunk upstairs, will you?
7 b Help me carry the trunk upstairs, would you?
8 a I don't trust David.
8 b I can't trust David.
9 a He's an athlete!
9 b He's some athlete!
10 a Did he have any brothers?
10 b Did he not have any brothers?
11 a She must have met him.
11 b She might have met him.
12 a John can't have understood.
12 b John may not have understood.

4 Make these requests sound more polite for a formal situation.

a Where is the post office?
b Put the bags on the table.
c Give me your tickets.
d Lend me your bike.
e Don't smoke here.

5 Make these statements sound less certain and more tentative.

a I'll see you tomorrow.
b I'll buy a new car if I can afford one.
c I wonder if you could lend me £10.
d Jill may have already left for the theatre.
e She can't have failed.

Vocabulary: Adverbs of manner

When acting in a play, it is very important, of course, to convey how your character is feeling through your words and actions. Here are some adverbs which suggest how someone feels as well as describing how something is done.

> angrily anxiously bitterly cheerfully confidently desperately eagerly excitedly furiously gladly gloomily gratefully happily helplessly impatiently miserably nervously passionately proudly reluctantly sadly shyly sincerely unhappily wearily

1 Divide the adverbs listed above into two or more groups – in any way that seems logical to you.

Compare your groupings with those of other students.

dancing passionately

2 Choose one of the actions below.

> walk round the room
> write something on a piece of paper
> greet a friend   look out of the window
> get on a plane   dance with somebody
> do some studying   watch TV

Now choose one of the adverbs. Mime doing the action in the style of the adverb. Can the other students guess the action and the adverb?

3 Although many adverbs end in *-ly*, there are some that do not. There are also some adjectives which end *-ly*.

Are the following words adjectives or adverbs? Note that they may be both.

> fast   poorly   doubtless   sickly   long
> miserly   hardly   daily   shortly
> wrong   loud   fortnightly   straight
> barely   kindly   late   quick   tight

If a word above is only either an adverb or an adjective, what form does it have as an adjective or an adverb (if it has an equivalent one)?

4 Choose five or six of the adverbs from Exercises 1 and 3 that you would particularly like to learn. Think about times when you have said or done something in this manner. Write a sentence using the adverb about this time.

For example, *I dropped wearily into bed at the end of the day spent walking on the hills* or *I asked shyly whether he would like to go to the party with me.*

dancing proudly

dancing gloomily

Speaking: Expressing feeling when you speak

1 ▭ Listen to the tape. Which mood do you think each speaker is in?

> angry   sad   happy   confused   afraid
> impatient   bored   excited

How does the person's voice suggest what mood he or she is in?

2 ▭ Listen to the tape again. Repeat the words after the speaker, conveying the same mood.

Would you use your voice in similar ways to convey emotion in your language?

NINE WAYS OF SAYING YES

No one has yet described all the nuances of meaning which can be conveyed by the intonation system. Even if we restrict the example to a single word (*yes*), and a single context (*Will you marry me?*), it proves difficult to capture everything that is involved. (The accent represented here is RP, p. 365. The direction of pitch movement is shown between two parallel lines, which represent the upper and lower limits of the speaker's pitch range. The commentary indicates the tone's general meaning, and parenthetically remarks on the likelihood of its use in nuptial circumstances.)

low fall
The most neutral tone; a detached, unemotional statement of fact. (Unlikely, though it could be quite a dramatic answer, after tempestuous preliminaries.)

full fall
Emotionally involved; the higher the onset of the tone, the more involved the speaker; choice of emotion (surprise, excitement, irritation) depends on the speaker's facial expression. (Possible, especially if accompanied by other tones of voice, such as breathiness.)

mid fall
Routine, uncommitted comment; detached and unexcited. ('I'm thinking about it.' Wedding bells seem unlikely.)

low rise
Facial expression important; with a 'happy' face, the tone is sympathetic and friendly; with a 'grim' face, it is guarded and ominous. (Neither makes particular sense, in this context, though the speaker might be thinking, 'What's the catch?')

full rise
Emotionally involved, often disbelief or shock, the extent of the emotion depending on the width of the tone. (Unlikely, though it might be used afterwards by the person popping the question, if he/she was not expecting to get a positive answer 'I don't believe you've said yes'.)

high rise
Mild query or puzzlement; often used in echoing what has just been said. (Unlikely, though it might be used to convey 'Are you sure you know what you're saying?')

level
Bored, sarcastic, ironic. (Unlikely. If used, it would have to mean something like 'If I really must' or 'I give up', or possibly, 'Here we go again, the same old routine'.)

fall-rise
A strongly emotional tone; a straight or 'negative' face conveys uncertainty, doubt, or tentativeness; a positive face conveys encouragement or urgency. (The latter is rather more likely than the former, which would be distinctly cagey, in this context. Maybe there are some conditions to be met.)

rise-fall
Strong emotional involvement; depending on the face, the attitude might be delighted, challenging, or complacent. (Very likely. With a bit of breathiness, the speaker can't wait.)

---

3 📼 Look at the text on the left and listen to the speaker on the tape illustrating the different ways in which the simple word *yes* can be pronounced.

4 📼 Listen again and repeat the word *yes* after the speaker, using your voice in the same way.

5 Follow these instructions.

1 On one piece of paper write down one of the adverbs of manner which you worked with in the previous vocabulary exercises. On another piece of paper write down a short sentence, anything that you might hear said in English.

2 Put all the adverb papers in one pile and all the sentences in another. Shuffle the papers in each pile.

3 Take it in turns to take one paper from each pile. Then read your sentence on one paper in the manner of the adverb on the other paper. The other students must try to guess what the adverb on your paper is.

The main aspects of language worked on in this unit are:	• listening to comedy • writing for your readers • countables and uncountables • ambiguity • study skills – looking back and forward

Warm-up: Humour

Discuss with two or three other students.

a What is your favourite television comedy (in your own country)? Why do you like it?

b Have you seen any English-language comedies on television or listened to any on the radio? If so, could you understand them? Did they make you laugh?

c Do you think that different nationalities have different senses of humour? Give examples to illustrate your opinion, if possible.

Listening: Comedy

It can be particularly difficult to understand comedy in a foreign language. In fact, some people say that the best kind of listening comprehension test for advanced students would be to play a tape of a set of jokes and to give marks to the candidates who laughed in the right places.

You are going to listen to an extract from a comedy programme from a popular series called *Yes, Prime Minister*. The series, which is reputedly very true to life, deals with the relationship between the Prime Minister and the civil service, the bureaucrats who provide the administrative back-up for the government. The members of the civil service in the UK do not change when the government changes and the civil servants in this series, the major one of whom is Sir Humphrey, Cabinet Secretary, believe that they really hold power while pretending to the politicians that it is they who are in charge.

In this programme, the Prime Minister is keen to make tax cuts but he knows that it will be hard to persuade the government and, in particular, the Treasury, to consent to this. The four characters in the scene which you will hear are the Prime Minister, Sir Humphrey, Bernard (the PM's secretary) and Peter Thorn (a doctor and junior Minister for Health).

The Prime Minister, Sir Humphrey and Bernard outside the Prime Minister's residence

1 To understand the comedy fully, you need to understand some terms relating to the political and social structure of Britain. What do the following mean? Find out if you are not sure.

the Treasury
the Cabinet
the (tobacco) lobby
the NHS
social security
an Act of Parliament

2 What is the relationship between the civil service and the government in Britain? How do you think that that affects the way civil servants and ministers behave towards each other? In your opinion what typifies the language of (a) bureaucrats and (b) politicians?

3 ▄ Listen to the extract from the programme and answer the following questions.

a Had the Prime Minister already read Peter Thorn's paper?
b What is the aim of Dr Thorn's proposal?
c Does the Prime Minister take his proposal seriously?
d Will the Prime Minister give him public support?
e Why does the Prime Minister want there to be a lot of publicity for the proposals?
f What does Sir Humphrey think of Dr Thorn's proposal?
g What adjective would you use to sum up the characters of each of the four people in this programme?
h What do you think will happen in the rest of the programme? Do you think Dr Thorn's proposal will succeed? Why or why not?

4 ▄ Listen to the programme again and then comment on the use of language in the following extracts from it. Say who is speaking and to whom. What exactly do they mean by what they are saying? Also comment on the way the speaker uses the English language.

a The Prime Minister often finds that a brief verbatim summary clarifies the emphasis and focuses on the salient points.
b Smoking must be stopped. And we will stop it. In due course. At the appropriate juncture. In the fullness of time.
c Please, don't misunderstand me. It's quite right, of course, that you should contemplate all proposals that come from your government. But no sane man would ever support it.
d It has been shown that if those extra 100,000 people had lived to a ripe old age they would have cost even more in pensions and social security than they did in medical treatment. So financially speaking, it's unquestionably better that they continue to die at about the present rate.
e When cholera killed 30,000 people in 1833, we got the Public Health Act. When smog killed two and a half thousand in 1952 we got the Clean Air Act. When a commercial drug kills half a dozen people, we get it withdrawn from sale. Cigarettes kill 100,000 people a year. And what do we get?

5 ▄ Read through the transcript of the programme on page 173, listening to the tape at the same time. Mark anything that you do not understand and ask other students in the class if they can help you. If they cannot help, ask the teacher to explain.

Grammar: Countable and uncountable nouns

1 Some nouns – like, for instance, *paper* and *a paper* – can be both countable and uncountable but with different meanings. Explain the difference between the following pairs of words.

a glass, a glass
b iron, an iron
c work, a work
d cloth, a cloth
e home, a home
f light, a light
g pepper, a pepper
h plant, a plant
i honey, a honey
j beauty, a beauty
k fish, a fish
l orange, an orange
m violet, a violet
n aid, an aid
o help, a help

2 Some words, like *politics,* end in *s* and look as if they should be plural words but they are, in fact, singular uncountable nouns. We can say *Politics is a dirty business,* for example. Here are the definitions of some more words like this. Solve the clues to complete the crossword.

ACROSS

1 a childhood illness with the symptoms of a rash and a high temperature

3 the scientific study of sound

5 the science of designing and constructing aeroplanes

6 track and field sports

7 the study of numbers, quantities and shapes

13 the skilful organisation of people and equipment so that work can be carried out effectively

14 the branch of physics which studies the forces acting on moving or stationary objects

15 the study of the ways in which countries are governed and power is acquired and wielded

16 an illness passed on by bites from infected animals

17 a kind of board game played with black and white pieces

DOWN

2 the study of language

4 the branch of medicine that is concerned with pregnancy and childbirth

5 a form of exercise which increases the amount of oxygen in your blood

8 the study of the production of wealth and the consumption of goods and services in a country

9 the scientific study of forces and qualities such as heat, light, sound, electricity, pressure and gravity and the way they affect objects

10 the study of Latin and Ancient Greek

11 a game played on a table with long sticks called cues and hard round coloured balls

12 the study of heredity

3 The majority of the words in Exercise 2 relate to branches of study. What is the name of the person who specialises in each of these fields? For example, a statistician specialises in statistics.

4 Note that one or two of the words in Exercise 2 are sometimes used as plural words. This is sometimes when they are referring not to a subject of study but to one person's activities or studies. For example, *Her politics tend to be reactionary.*

Fill in the blanks with *is* or *are* as appropriate. Use a dictionary to help you, if necessary.

a The acoustics in this hall .... terrible.

b Acoustics .... the study of sound.

c All the classics .... in this library.

d Classics .... not taught so much now as it used to be.

e Draughts .... one of my favourite games.

f Draughts .... a fact of life in most English houses.

g Government statistics .... not always reliable.

h Statistics .... a very difficult subject.

i The logistics of the situation .... complex.

j Logistics .... an important part of Jack's course.

k There .... a lot of mechanics studying on our course.

l There .... a lot of mechanics to do on our course.

Writing: Writing for your readers

It is very important, when you are writing something – in any language – to think about who you are writing for. Your potential audience affects both the style that you use and the content of what you say.

Peter Thorn would write differently about the harmful effects of smoking if he were writing for a professional journal like the *British Medical Journal* than if he were writing for, say, a popular newspaper like *The Sun*.

1 What style (for example, very formal or fairly informal) would be appropriate for an anti-smoking piece to be included in:

a a leaflet to go in doctors' waiting rooms?
b a magazine for 9 to 11-year-olds?
c a newsletter for people trying to give up smoking?
d a textbook for medical students?

2 Which of (a) to (d) above would the following extracts be most likely to come from? How do you know?

i Regular inhalation of nicotine has a deleterious effect on both the cardiovascular and the respiratory systems.
ii Julia Haines (33) tried the new patch which is supposed to get you over those first dreadful days when your body craves a cigarette so strongly that you think you will never resist.
iii The lungs of people who don't smoke are a nice fresh pink colour, but even someone who only smokes one or two a day has lungs that are a grimy black colour.
iv Remember that smoking affects not only smokers but also their families and colleagues.

3 Your task here is to do two pieces of writing on a similar topic but taking, probably, a rather different point of view in each.

The first piece of writing is a report on what you have learnt from your studies this year for either your boss or the headteacher of the college where you are studying. He or she may be able to give you some money to help you study more next year if you can show that you are a serious student who is benefiting from the educational opportunities offered. The second piece of writing is a letter to a close friend of yours who is considering doing the same course next year. You know that your friend is not keen on working hard and is mainly interested in the social and leisure opportunities offered by your place of study.

Follow these instructions.

1 Discuss with a partner what might be an appropriate style and content for each of these two pieces.
2 Plan your report and your letter.
3 Write the report and the letter.
4 Compare what you wrote with the work of other students in the class.

Vocabulary: Ambiguity

1 The Prime Minister refers to Peter Thorn's report as a *cigarette paper* and then decides it isn't a very good term to use. Why?

2 ⌦ Listen to the tape and read these verses from Roger McGough's poem *On and on and on.* Explain the pun in each verse.

Is a shoplifter
a giant
who goes around lifting shops?

Is a popsinger
a singer
who sings and then pops?

Is a big spender
a spender
who's exceedingly big?

Is a pig farmer
really
a land-owning pig?

Does a baby-sitter
really
sit on tiny tots?

Is a pot-holer
a gunman
who shoots holes in pots?

Is a monster crane
a ferocious
man-eating crane?

Is a train-spotter
an artist
who paints spots on trains?

Is a batsman
a man
who is completely bats?

Is a cat-burglar
a thief
who likes stealing cats?

Is a light bulb
a bulb
that is light as a feather?

Does an opera buff
sing
in the altogether?

Is a slip road
a road
that is covered in ice?

Are price cuts
wounds
you get at a price?

Is a waiting room
a room
that patiently waits?

Is a gatekeeper's
hobby
collecting gates?

Is sandpaper
used
for wrapping up sand?

If you lay down
your arms
can you still lend a hand?

Is a sick bed
a bed
that is feeling unwell?

Is a crime wave
a criminal's
wave of farewell?

Is a horseman …

3 Do any ambiguous expressions like these exist in your own language? If so, try translating them into English.

4 With a partner, make up some verses of your own like those of Roger McGough's, based on ambiguous expressions in English.

Study skills: Looking back and forward

Now you are coming to the end of this book it is a good point to look back at the English learning you have done on this course and to look forward to your plans for the future. It is important to appreciate just how much progress you have made and to ensure that you not only do not lose what you have already mastered but that you also keep on learning.

With other students discuss these questions.

a In what ways is your English now better than when you started this course? (You may be able to look back at some early homework or you may have a recording of yourself to help you recognise your progress.)

b Where do you feel that you now need to make most progress?

c How can you help to maximise your progress – both in and out of class?

Tapescripts

Unit 2 Listening Exercise 1

Here's the news at 11 o'clock on Tuesday January the 20th.

At least 45 people are now known to have died in the California earthquake. The US president is to visit the area today to see for himself the scene of the devastation. It was the worst earthquake that the country has suffered for over three decades. Thousands of residents have spent a second night camped out in parks and gardens. Many areas are still without water or electricity and estimates put the repair bill at over 7 billion dollars.

The day after and South Hill is slowly creaking back into gear even though there's nowhere to go. As aftershocks rumble on, shock is sinking in – the horror over the dead and injured and the hundreds made homeless. Insurance companies face the inevitable rush for claims. But only one in five of the local population is insured against earthquakes and so thousands of people have lost everything.

Figures out today show that retail sales last year were worse than expected. Despite hopes of a December boom, sales actually dropped. And there has been a sharp rise in inflation. The annual rate went up by half of one percent to 1.9%. The Chancellor claimed that the economic situation is still positive and that there is every reason to believe that we are already well on our way out of the recession.

English Aeroplanes are to cut a further 400 jobs at their Birmingham and Manchester plants. Last week they said that 75 workers in Liverpool would lose their jobs. The jobless total in the country now stands at 2.8 million, an increase of 110,000 over the figures for January last year.

Crime figures released today show that illegal drugs worth more than £500 billion were seized by customs and excise officers last year. Record hauls of cocaine and amphetamines were captured. Customs officers have succeeded in breaking up a number of large drug rings and over 100 arrests have been made.

And that's it. More news headlines in an hour.

Unit 8 Listening Exercise 1

A: Anyway it was my third appearance in court … it had dragged on for ages and ages and I was unbelievably nervous, you know, I was sweating, crying, I couldn't speak, I couldn't complete a sentence …

B: Tell us what you were in court for.

A: Oh, oh, well , yes it, it was well it was a few months before … I was arrested for assaulting a police officer in the line of his duty. And um …

C: I can't believe that.

A: I know it's it is very hard to believe, isn't it when you look at me? I mean …

B: How did it happen?

A: He was twice my size.

C: You mean you actually assaulted is that …

A: Well, I, no, I pleaded innocent.

C: Well, yes, of course.

A: Not guilty. The fact of the matter was, I'd parked my car – I never usually drive into the West End but it was raining and I didn't have child care arranged at home and I had to get into the West End to do a job very very quickly … so I drove in and I found a meter. I put my money in the meter – £1.20 … and it didn't work, and I know it's illegal to use a meter that doesn't work to park your car, so having put my money in and parked my car, I wrote a note and left it in the window explaining to whoever that I had put money in and it appears it isn't working, and I thought I was being a dutiful citizen.

B: Yes, you were.

C: Very considerate, actually.

A: I also said I was only going to be away for 25 minutes … which was exactly, exactly the case.

B: Did you have the children with you?

A: No, I didn't. I had the car seats in the back of the car which I thought might put them off a bit.

C: Make them sympathetic.

A: But this police officer wasn't interested and when I came back to my car I was clamped. There was a big, you know, that yellow clamp around the wheel!

C: What a nightmare!

A: And it had nearly … in fact you know I had so much time that I'd bought a sandwich on my way back from the job so I knew I, I wasn't in a hurry and I had my umbrella and my basket and this police officer was so rude to me, I indicated that I'd written a note and he said 'Well everybody else who parks on meters is a liar, why, why should I believe that you're not?' and proceeded to carry on clamping the next car. He ignored me. I was asking how I could reverse the situation, who I should write to, who I should telephone, was there somewhere I could go and he wouldn't, he wouldn't even look at me.

C: Yes. Mm.

A: So, I snatched the clamp card that he was about to give to the next car, to stick it on, I snatched it from his hands and he arrested me on the spot because I'd had physical contact with him. After he arrested me I did hit him with my chicken mayonnaise sandwich …

C: Brilliant!

A: I didn't get a dry cleaning … I thought I might get a bill from the Metropolitan Police for dry cleaning of his uniform but that didn't happen but I became an hysterical woman there and then …

B: I'm not surprised!

A: … because I just couldn't believe it and I was calling to people to witness this situation which was so ludicrous, and he called two colleagues and a van to take me away, so you can imagine the state I was in, and of course they took me down to the charge room – which was 200 yards away in fact – but they had to take me in a van because they wanted to make a display.

C: We're laughing now but that at the time that must have been …

A: It was dreadful! And then of course I had to phone my boyfriend and say 'You won't believe where I am …'

C: Did he laugh when you told him? I mean, no, obviously he didn't laugh …

A: No, it got worse, it actually got worse, they actually offered me … two other police officers in the charge room offered me a caution, which I should have accepted but I was very ignorant of the law. I knew nothing about the law really and I was so angry with this police officer that I said, 'No, I'm going to see him in court!' And of course I didn't realise it would have to be a magistrates' court because it's … any assault of a police officer cannot be tried in front of a jury … it's a magistrates' court, and it's treated very seriously indeed. I could have got sent down, in fact, for a short period of time. Well I got a wonderful barrister who made mincemeat of the police officer and his ridiculous statement. But the most embarrassing …

B: Satisfying?

A: Yes, it was very satisfying. The most embarrassing thing was that my father turned up in court and my father thinks that I'm an innocent young little girl still. Really, he's never come to terms with me growing up, and he's never heard me swear and he had to sit in court and hear these things that I'd said to the police officer, which were all true, in fact, absolutely true, I didn't deny any of that. But he couldn't bear it, he was … it was worse, watching my father seeing his dream of his little girl shattered. The reality of the case …

B: Has it changed your relationship?

A: Yes, I think it has, actually, I think it's improved it. I think he's realised that he's had to let go of me …

B: He knows you're grown up now.

C: I should think there was a number of people in court that were cheering.

A: Well, my brother, who's a comedian, said he wouldn't miss it for the world. He's used it for material for his stand up

C: I think that you were speaking for millions of motorists who've been clamped.

A: The other thing, of course, was that I got the clamp reversed because I was in the right. I got the money back on the clamp.

B: You …

A: I proved that I was in the right; they checked the meter and everything, but the fact that I had actually physically touched a police officer and was seen to be in an hysterical state after he'd arrested me condemned me, and the judge couldn't believe that I hadn't hit him before – and I admitted hitting him after the arrest so I got done.

B: So did you have to pay a fine?

A: I got a fine of £50 and a conditional discharge.

C: Did they replace your chicken mayonnaise sandwich?

A: No they didn't, but the barrister asked me to appear in court dressed exactly as I was on the day – with the mac and I had an umbrella in my right hand, which I didn't use which at the time I thought was exercising, you know, considerable restraint …

B: Yes, absolutely!

A: Yes, if I'd wanted to hit him, I'd have used my umbrella, not the sandwich but he had me go and buy a sandwich, the exact same sandwich from the exact bar!

C: A reconstruction. An exact reconstruction. It should have been wet as well …

A: It was very amusing in retrospect, but at the time …

B: And it must have dragged on for a long time.

A: Yes, it was my third appearance, everything gets postponed in court, they haven't got the right papers …

C: But that's a big …

Unit 10 Listening Exercise 1

JANE: Well, I'm sorry, I'm sorry, I've got to say this. I just think life is still much easier today if you're a man.

CHRIS: I agree.

JANE: It really is. Getting work is easier, the whole thing is …

DAVID: Well yes but, I mean, it does depend. You talk about work but … things are expected or society expects certain things of a man at work, you know the problem of promotion, being a breadwinner at home …

JANE: Being promoted is a problem. It's a problem if you're a woman, you don't get promoted, men get promoted over you.

DAVID: Well, that's what I'm saying.

CHRIS: Society may expect it but it's a male society, it's a male-dominated society. Do you not agree?

KATE: I think things are changing rapidly and that may have been true 20 years ago but it certainly isn't now.

JANE: Oh, I'm sorry.

KATE: I can't agree with you.

JANE: I can't agree with you. It's supposed to be that things are changing rapidly but I think things are just the same as they were 20 years ago.

KATE: We as women have much more choice now than our mothers' generation did. We can choose to have a family and a career.

CHRIS: Yes, but in my opinion that is two jobs, isn't it?

KATE: Yes.

CHRIS: Having a family … it's not as simple, it's not a little bag that you carry around with you, it's an enormous job, it's two jobs in fact. That and work. So why can't a man take on the two jobs?

JANE: Absolutely.

DAVID: I think a man does take on the two jobs.

CHRIS: Rubbish.

DAVID: No, no, no, no. Hear me out. If you've got pressure at work, you also have a pressure at home of being the head of the family, of supporting the family, there's a, you know, there are two jobs.

JANE: Excuse me, why do you have to be the one who supports the family, or be the head of it? Surely the couple – if it is a man and a woman raising a family, it isn't always that of course – why aren't they both the head of the family?

DAVID: Well, yes indeed, yes indeed. I mean, let's change it. Would that were the case. But I'm saying now is that is what is depicted by society, you know that.

KATE: I'm sure it's up to the couple themselves to choose the power roles …

JANE: Oh, I don't think so.

KATE: that best work for the family. But in my own experience, we both work, we share responsibilities for the children. There are things that my husband will do and other things that I will do, but I certainly don't feel short-changed in any way. I just can't agree with you. I think your argument is tired and old.

JANE: I would like to get back to what I was saying in the first place about about the ability to get jobs. I still think it's much easier for men to get jobs and men are promoted above women.

CHRIS: Mm.

JANE: And I've got a case in point. My sister is a palaeontologist, she's about to have a baby, she's sorted out the child care which she's going to be using when the baby is born. And she has not got the job. It's gone to a man who is not nearly as well qualified as she is.

KATE: Excuse me, it was her choice to have a child.

JANE: Yes, it was her choice to have a child. But it was also her choice to do the job. And she is better qualified than anybody in that part of the country to do this job. But she didn't get it because she also wanted to have a child. Why shouldn't she have a child as well?

CHRIS: Yes. Quite. I agree. I'd like to know. I'd be interested to know if her husband, who presumably would have been involved in the choice to have a baby as well, I think you'll find, if they, her husband and she had discussed who was going to give up a job?

JANE: Oh, yes.

KATE: It's biological, isn't it? I mean, a husband doesn't have to take off six months to breast feed the baby, it's biological.

JANE: But he is actually taking six months off work in order to look after the baby so that she can start preparing for the job, well if she got it, but in fact now she's not got the job.

KATE: Well, that's his choice again. I just think that we have a lot more choice now.

JANE: I can't agree with you. I'm sorry, I mean, really, if you came on to this earth again, would you really choose to be a woman?

KATE: Yes, absolutely, without a doubt. Would you prefer to stay as a man or be a woman?

DAVID: Hmm. Hypothetical question.

Unit 11 Listening Exercise 1

INTERVIEWER: Excuse me, madam. I wonder if you could help me. How has life changed since you were a child? For better or worse?

WOMAN: Oh, I think, I think, it's changed for the better. Really, there are, well, of course, I mean, one can say it's better and worse in different ways but basically I think things are better now. I don't think there's so much poverty in this country, in the world. And from a sort of personal point of view, there are so many things to help you in the house for instance. I mean, I've got a washing machine and a hoover, you know, and my mother didn't have any of those things. She used to wash everything by hand and she had to use a brush and dustpan and she had to get up very early to light fires. We have central heating which we can just switch on. And I think on the whole young people have a better time of it today. I mean, they have more chance to to travel and see the world. I think in my young day people didn't really go very much further than their own home town you know, and people now as a matter of course go abroad for their holidays or to work sometimes so I think I think it's changed for the better really.

INTERVIEWER: Thank you. Excuse me, sir, could I trouble you for a moment?

MAN: Yeah, yeah.

INTERVIEWER: Would you say that the quality of life is improving or deteriorating?

MAN: Oh, deteriorating, definitely deteriorating.

INTERVIEWER: Why's that?

MAN: Oh, well, I mean, you know. Look at us. You know, we've come to London for the day here and the time was when you could walk in the park and have a good bit of fresh air but you know the pollution's terrible, the fumes and the taxis and things and you know, I mean, it's not just that, it's the overpopulation, you know, violence and crime. Oh no, it's definitely deteriorating, I'd say.

INTERVIEWER: Thank you.

Unit 14 Listening Exercise 2

Hello, I'm Penny Mason and I edit the Problem Page at *Weekly News* and I'm very glad you've rung to find out more about how to cope with loneliness. It's one of the worst feelings in the world, isn't it? All around you everyone seems to look so purposeful, doing things, talking to friends and so on; but has it ever occurred to you that however happy they seem on the surface, lots of people do actually feel terribly lonely inside? You're not the only one. Indeed, it's thought that there are over two million lonely people in this country alone. But how are you going to tackle the problem?

Firstly, try to separate your feelings of loneliness from yourself. If you broke your leg, you wouldn't then draw the conclusion that you were a broken personality, would you? So if you're lonely don't feel yourself as an unlovable isolated person. Don't get into that vicious circle which starts with the idea that *I'm lonely because I have no friends* leading on to *I've got no friends because no one likes me* leading on to *No one likes me because I'm horrible.* This is muddled thinking; it's just not true. You are you, and you are loveable and always will be.

Loneliness is something separate that you're suffering from temporarily like the flu. Tackle it bravely and practically as you would any other problem.

Secondly, take the initiative. Ask people round for coffee, a drink, a meal or whatever. Everyone's flattered to receive an invitation. Make a habit of it. Resolve to have someone round at least once a week, even if it's just a neighbour you don't know very well. Chances are she's just as lonely as you.

Thirdly, join some outside activities whether it's a choir, drama class, rambling association, local sports club, evening class or even your local political party. Your library's got details of all the local activities. I know you're thinking that that's a corny, old hat idea. Like everyone else, I've felt lonely at times and when a friend suggested joining clubs or evening classes, I cringed too. But she turned out to be right. Maybe you won't make friends at evening class but you may well bump into an old acquaintance on the bus there. Maybe you won't meet people over the counter if you get a Saturday job in a shop but you might make friends with people behind the counter. What I'm saying is that you may not find company from the direction you're expecting it but you'll invariably find your loneliness relieved from other surprising sources. But only if you get out in the first place. You'll never meet anyone if you sit behind closed doors.

If it's a partner you're after, then try a dating agency. If you follow up lonely hearts ads, do exercise caution, won't you? And if you ever feel desperately lonely, the Samaritans are always there to help. You'll find them in the phone book.

I do hope these thoughts have helped and if you want more information, addresses, helpful book titles and further ideas, then send me a stamped addressed envelope at *Weekly News* and I'll send you my leaflet on loneliness. If you're lonely, you might also be interested in my leaflets on voluntary work, bereavement, penfriends, depression and assertion or just drop me a line and I'll reply.

I'm looking forward to hearing from you.

Unit 20 Listening Exercise 1

Now anyone familiar with the scholarly research on gender differences in language will immediately recognise the source of this magazine article, a book by the American linguist, Robin Lakoff, published in 1975 under the title, *Language and Women's Place.* Lakoff was the first linguist to publish a whole book on the subject of gender differences in the use of English and her book was influential because it opened up a whole new line of enquiry.

What Lakoff suggested was the existence of a distinctive register in English called 'women's language'. The alternative, by the way, is not men's language, it's neutral language. The difference between neutral language and women's language is that women's language lacks force, authority and confidence. It's full of hedge words like 'perhaps', 'sort of' and 'I'm not really sure'. It's full of tags, rising intonation which makes statements into question, trivial words and polite expressions. Women use this language, Lakoff suggests, because they were taught as little girls that it was feminine or ladylike. But what's charming in a little girl becomes irritating in a grown woman trying to make her way in the world. Women who talk the way women are supposed to won't be taken seriously as competent professionals because the language itself is neither competent nor professional.

This argument in the last 20 years has provided a very strong rationale for courses designed to change women's speech habits and make them more effective or powerful communicators. As I said before, such courses might look like a classic example of linguistic findings being applied to a real world problem, the problem of women's speech style. If we believe in gender equality, perhaps we should be applauding.

Unit 20 Listening Exercise 2

But those of us who work in the field of language and gender studies are unlikely to be applauding for several reasons. One is that, although Lakoff deserves credit as a pioneer who brought the subject of gender differences in language to the attention of a wide audience, she can't be given much credit for the quality of her research on the subject since she did no empirical research at all. Her book really belongs to a very old tradition of anecdotal speculation about women backed up by no real evidence. Those who've set out to gather the evidence since 1975 have found a much more complicated picture than Lakoff suggested.

There are differences in speech style between women and men, though like all social differences they're not absolute or without exception. We're dealing here with generalisations, averages. Nevertheless, even having said that, there is no such thing as a women's language. On one hand, the linguistic differences between different women are as great as the differences between women and men. On the other hand, many differences that seem to be connected with gender are actually more closely connected with an intervening variable such as social status or situational context.

The way women are said to speak often turns out to be the way people speak in a particular setting or the way people speak when they are in a subordinate position. Because in most societies women tend to be found in some settings more than men and vice versa and also women tend to occupy low status positions more than men, the variables of status, setting and gender can very easily get conflated. When this is done by academic theorists, it is a regrettable error. But when it becomes the basis for real world interventions, it has more serious implications.

If women's generally low status, for example, is the reason for certain features of their speech style, and not as the trainers would have it, the other way round, then obviously training women in a different style of speech is not going to solve the problem. At the same time, the theory of women's language gives employers and others a justification for women's continuing low status, that women don't get on as well as men because they're not effective communicators. This is a stereotype and a damaging one for women.

That brings me to the second problem with Lakoff's work and with training materials based on the idea of women's language as an inferior register. I've already said that Lakoff over-estimated the degree to which women differ from men, but in addition, later researchers have suggested she was wrong in her very negative assessment of so-called women's language. Even if all women in all situations did speak in the ways Lakoff claimed, which, to repeat, is very far from being the case, you would still have to pose the question: What's wrong with the way women speak?

Unit 22 Listening Exercise 1

She seemed such a sweet old dear. As I gulped down the last of her hot tea, I almost wished we were about to do something clean and honest and decent. Like an armed raid on Dr Barnado's. You see, she didn't really have rats in her attic, and never would have – not until me and Knuckles got up there, anyway. What she *did* have up there – according to the grapevine – was a fortune in ready cash …

I emptied a handful of crumbs into an onyx ashtray and motioned Knuckles to pick up the traps. Her ladyship got the message and rose gracefully to her feet.

'It's a long climb to the top – such a huge house!' she apologised. 'The upper part of the building is somewhat dusty – I no longer employ servants …'

I grinned inwardly at this last bit of information and we followed the old girl up a succession of wide, marbled stairways. On the top landing a ladder stretched up to the attic. Knuckles clambered up this and slid back the heavy steel bolts on the trap door.

Her ladyship smiled. 'Sir Percy, my late husband, was convinced that a burglar might be tempted to - ah – drop in on us …' she explained.

I nodded. One way and another, Sir Percy seemed to have had a thing about burglars.

With its thick stone walls, solid oak woodwork and barred windows, the place was like a fortress.

Unit 22 Listening Exercise 3

I shot up the ladder and lowered the trap door behind me. Knuckles lit a couple of candles, brushed the cobwebs from the corner of a tea chest and sank down heavily.

'Supposing it's not in 'ere,' he demanded, jerking a thumb over his shoulder at the jumble of lockers and boxes.

'It's here all right!' I assured him confidently. 'Couple of months ago the old girl was rushed to the hospital for an emergency op. As she came round from the gas she murmured, "It's in the attic!" over and over again – "It's in the attic!" '

I groped my way across to a hardboard partition and beckoned him to fetch over a candle.

'Some sort of office …' I guessed. 'A retreat. Somewhere the late Sir Percy could gloat over his relics in privacy. Collected bones by the looks of it – bones and fossils …'

'Funny old geezer!' Knuckles said. 'How did he die?'

I knew the answer to that, too. I do my homework.

'He got involved with another woman – big scandal. Ended up getting lost on a climbing expedition!' I snatched a cassette player from his fingers and pushed him away. 'The money's not in here – we split up and turn the attic inside out …'

Unit 22 Listening Exercise 4

We grafted hard for a full hour without finding anything. You could have hidden a double-decker bus in that darned attic, I can tell you. Every chest, case and biscuit tin had to be pulled apart, every loose floorboard investigated. I was just thinking that Madam might have got suspicious and phoned the law when I heard this yell from Knuckles. And right then his voice didn't sound like the tinkling of a cash register. I stumbled across to find him arched over a heap of rags in the corner.

'It's a body, isn't it?' he said accusingly, brushing cold sweat from his eyes. Something in his expression told me that he suddenly wanted to be a long way away. Somewhere nice and hospitable – like the moon.

'Sir Percy? Yeah that figures,' I replied, trying hard to keep my cool. 'Her ladyship knew he was giving her the run-around – and that's a pretty good motive!'

'You mean she croaked him?'

'Why not? But not up here – no signs of a struggle …' I lit a cigarette and studied him thoughtfully. 'It adds up, doesn't it? She arranged for him to get lost – permanently. A climbing expedition … up to his own attic!'

'Oh, Gawd 'elp us …' Knuckles breathed. Suddenly his tone hardened. 'You berk! She said it was in the attic, didn't she? Not the money – the perishing body!'

I backed away a fraction, fully expecting him to lash out at me. But he didn't. He glared at me a moment, and then thumped his way over to the trap door.

'You flaming great berk!' he shouted, and slammed the door shut after him. A couple of minutes later, I heard the sound of his van as it tore down the drive, and I relaxed.

Unit 22 Listening Exercise 5

The great thing about being a pro, I thought, is that you've learned to improvise. Like they say, as one door closes another one opens – and life, to a good pro, is a series of open doors. The trouble with Knuckles – and millions like him – was that they never stopped to think.

To someone like me, a body in the attic was worth money in the bank. Whichever way you looked at it,

her ladyship had been a very naughty girl. Concealing bodies in lofts wasn't exactly croquet, after all. It was big trouble.

But I must admit I spent a long time trying to figure out how Sir Percy died. Contrary to what I'd told Knuckles, I didn't really suspect the old girl of killing him.

You see, she couldn't have croaked him in the attic – she'd obviously never been up there. And if she'd croaked him in the house – how had she got his body up the ladder?

At the end of my fourth cigarette I gave up. It didn't seem to matter. I was just trying to fix a suitable figure for blackmail when I heard the sound of her ladyship's laughter. It terminated abruptly as she rammed home the bolts on the trap door …

Unit 24 Listening Exercise 3

BERNARD: Dr Thorn, Prime Minister.

PRIME MINISTER: Peter, come in, sit down. Now you wanted to talk to me about …

DR THORN: Cigarettes. You read my paper?

PRIME MINISTER: Yes, absolutely.

DR THORN: How did you react?

PRIME MINISTER: Er, well, I wonder if you could summarise it in your own words.

DR THORN: Those were my own words.

PRIME MINISTER: Yes, yes, exactly, of course, but …

BERNARD: The Prime Minister often finds that a brief verbatim summary clarifies the emphasis and focuses on the salient points.

PRIME MINISTER: The salient points. Precisely.

DR THORN: Well, briefly, I'm proposing that the government should take action to eliminate smoking, a complete ban on all cigarette sponsorship and advertising even at the point of sale, £50 million to be spent on anti-smoking publicity, ban smoking in all public places and progressive deterrent tax rises over the next five years until a packet of 20 costs about the same as a bottle of whisky.

PRIME MINISTER: Isn't that rather drastic?

DR THORN: Absolutely. It should reduce smoking by at least 80%. 90% if we're lucky, and drive the tobacco companies out of business.

PRIME MINISTER: Yes, but, Peter, of course you know I agree with you basically. Smoking must be stopped. No question. And we will stop it. In due course. At the appropriate juncture. In the fullness of time.

DR THORN: You mean, forget it.

PRIME MINISTER: Oh no, absolutely not. But we must be realists. You and I weren't born yesterday.

DR THORN: No and we didn't die yesterday.

PRIME MINISTER: No. What?

DR THORN: 300 people did. Prematurely. As a result of smoking. 100,000 deaths a year at least.

PRIME MINISTER: It's appalling. But you know what would happen if I took this to the Cabinet. You know what the Treasury would say?

DR THORN: YES. They'd say that smoking brings in four billion pounds a year in revenue and we can't manage without it.

PRIME MINISTER: And you can't beat the Treasury.

DR THORN: No, not with financial arguments. But this is a moral argument.

PRIME MINISTER: Yes, but … wait a minute. I've got an idea. This could be a way to beat the Treasury.

DR THORN: You mean, you'll support me?

PRIME MINISTER: You've made your point. We'll give it a try. I'll even read your report. Again. This could be very interesting. Thank you very much indeed.

DR THORN: But will you support me?

PRIME MINISTER: Well, not publicly. It would undermine my position, undermine the argument if I were to support you from the start. I have to be seen as the impartial judge who's swayed by the force of the argument.

DR THORN: Yes, I see that.

PRIME MINISTER: But off the record, I'd like to see this pushed very hard, very hard indeed. I'd like to see you make some speeches on it. Peter, thank you very much indeed. Thank you for your cigarette paper, your paper on …

DR THORN: Thank you, Prime Minister?

BERNARD: Is this serious, Prime Minister?

PRIME MINISTER: What do you mean, Bernard?

BERNARD: Well, it's always been the practice in the past to discourage anti-smoking speeches by ministers and not to print or distribute their speeches if they make them.

PRIME MINISTER: Well, I want Peter's speeches printed and distributed. I want everybody to know.

BERNARD: Yes, Prime Minister. Do you think you'll win this one? The tobacco lobby is incredibly powerful.

PRIME MINISTER: Well, some you win, some you lose, Bernard. And this one I shall definitely lose.

BERNARD: Why?

PRIME MINISTER: If you were the Treasury, which would you rather do without – one and a half million in tax cuts or four billion pounds in lost tobacco tax revenues?

BERNARD: The tax cut, it's smaller.

PRIME MINISTER: Exactly. That's what I want and that's what I shall get.

BERNARD: Oh, it's Sir Humphrey. Can he have a word?

PRIME MINISTER: Yes, of course.

BERNARD: Come in, please.

SIR HUMPHREY: Ah, Prime Minister.

PRIME MINISTER: Humphrey.

SIR HUMPHREY: I was just wondering, did you have an interesting chat with Dr Thorn?

PRIME MINISTER: Yes, he proposed the elimination of smoking.

SIR HUMPHREY: By a campaign of mass hypnosis perhaps?

PRIME MINISTER: By raising tobacco taxes sky-high and simultaneously banning all advertising including at point of sale. Don't you think his position is admirably moral?

SIR HUMPHREY: Moral perhaps but extremely silly. No man in his right mind could possibly contemplate such a proposal.

PRIME MINISTER: I'm contemplating it.

SIR HUMPHREY: Yes, of course, Prime Minister. Please, don't misunderstand me. It's quite right, of course, that you should contemplate all proposals that come from your government. But no sane man would ever support it.

PRIME MINISTER: I'm supporting it.

SIR HUMPHREY: And quite right too, Prime Minister. You see the only little problem is that the tax on tobacco is a major source of revenue for the government.

PRIME MINISTER: It's also a major source of death from killer diseases.

SIR HUMPHREY: Yes, indeed, but no definite causative link has ever been proved, has it?

PRIME MINISTER: The statistics are undeniable.

SIR HUMPHREY: Statistics. You can prove anything with statistics.

PRIME MINISTER: Even the truth. It says here that smoking-related diseases cost the NHS £165 million a year.

SIR HUMPHREY: Yes, but we have been into that. It has been shown that if those extra 100,000 people had lived to a ripe old age they would have cost us even more in pensions and social security than they did in medical treatment. So financially speaking, it's unquestionably better that they continue to die at about the present rate.

PRIME MINISTER: When cholera killed 30,000 people in 1833, we got the Public Health Act. When smog killed two and a half thousand people in 1952 we got the Clean Air Act. A commercial drug kills half a dozen people, we get it withdrawn from sale. Cigarettes kill 100,000 people a year. And what do we get?

SIR HUMPHREY: £4 billion a year.

Phonetic symbols

LONG VOWELS

iː	ɑː	ɔː	uː	ɜː
sheep	farm	horse	shoe	bird
/ʃiːp/	/£fɑːm/	/£hɔːs/	/ʃuː/	/£bɜːd/
	/$fɑːrm/	/$hɔːrs/		/$bɜːrd/

SHORT VOWELS

ɪ	e	æ	ʌ	(Br)ɒ	ʊ	ə	(Am)ɚ
ship	head	hat	cup	sock	foot	above	mother
/ʃɪp/	/hed/	/hæt/	/kʌp/	/£sɒk/	/fʊt/	/əˈbʌv/	/$ˈmʌð·ɚ/

DIPHTHONGS (Two vowel sounds together)

eɪ	aɪ	ɔɪ	aʊ	(Br)əʊ	(Am)oʊ	(Br)ɪə	(Br)ea	(Br)ʊɜ
day	eye	boy	mouth	nose	nose	ear	hair	pure
/deɪ/	/aɪ/	/bɔɪ/	/maʊθ/	/£nəʊz/	/$noʊz/	/£ɪəʳ/	/£heaʳ/	/£pjʊəʳ/

CONSONANTS

	p	t	k	f	θ	s	ʃ	tʃ
voiceless	pen	town	cat	fish	think	say	she	cheese
	/pen/	/taʊn/	/kæt/	/fɪʃ/	/θɪŋk/	/seɪ/	/ʃiː/	/tʃiːz/

	b	d	g	v	ð	z	ʒ	dʒ
voiced	book	day	give	very	the	zoo	vision	jump
	/bʊk/	/deɪ/	/gɪv/	/ˈver·ɪ/	/ðə/	/zuː/	/vɪʒn/	/dʒʌmp/

l	r	j	w	m	n	ŋ	h
look	run	yes	we	moon	name	sing	hand
/lʊk/	/rʌn/	/jes/	/wiː/	/muːn/	/neɪm/	/sɪŋ/	/hænd/

Acknowledgements

The author would like to thank the following people: editors Helena Gomm, Barbara Thomas, Liz Sharman and Lindsay White; designers Nick Newton and Randell Harris; everybody at Cambridge University Press for making this book possible.

The author and publishers would like to thank the teachers and students who trialled and commented on the material and whose feedback was invaluable.

The authors and publishers are grateful to the authors, publishers and others who have given permission for the use of copyright material identified in the text. It has not been possible to identify the sources of all the material used and in such cases the publishers would welcome information from copyright owners. Apologies are expressed for any omissions.

The Observer for the text on p. 7 by Philip French, © *The Observer*; the text on p. 16 is from *The Essential Anatomy of Britain: Democracy in Crisis* by Anthony Sampson, copyright © 1993 by Anthony Sampson, reprinted by permission of Harcourt Brace & Company and Hodder & Stoughton Ltd; The BBC for the brochures on p. 18 and for the extracts on the cassette (Unit 10 and 12) from *Sporting Gaffes*, reproduced courtesy of the BBC; Cambridge University Press for the dictionary entry on p. 19 from *Cambridge International Dictionary of English*, for the extracts on pp. 20, 21, 38 and 261 from *Cambridge Encyclopedia of the EnglishLanguage* by D. Crystal, ; Addison Wesley Longman for the dictionary entries on p. 19 from *Longman Lexicon of Contemporary English*, reprinted by permission of Addison Wesley Longman Ltd; HarperCollins Publishers for the three lists on p. 19 from *Collins Cobuild English Grammar*, published 1990, for quotations g–h on p. 32 from *Collins Thematic Dictionary of Quotations* by Robert Andrew, for the book cover of *4.50 from Paddington* by Agatha Christie on p. 136 and for the text on p. 138 (top) from *Language and Women's Place* by Robin Lakoff; Uni Mitsubishi Pencil Company UK Ltd, Seiko UK Ltd and Cafédirect Ltd for the advertisements on p. 26; CNFM radio station, Task Force Recruitment, Rossiter's, Specter and Grant, Kingsway Golf Centre and Ben's Cookies for the radio adverts on the cassette (Unit 4); No Master's Cooperative for the recording on the cassette and Voice Publishing for the music and lyrics of 'Make it Mend it' (arranged Coope, Boyes and Simpson) on p.37; BMG Entertainment International UK & Ireland Ltd for the recording on the cassette and The International Music Network Ltd for the lyrics of the song 'The End of the World' by Skeeter Davis on p. 37; Uniquity for the advertisements on p. 43; *The Times* for the text on p. 53, the review on *Forrest Gump* on p. 130 and for the revision exercise no 1 p. 38 in the Teacher's Book © The Times Newspapers Ltd; Tony Buzan for the text on p. 56 and the revision exercise no 4 pp. 150–151 in the Teacher's Book from *Use Your Head*; Virgin Publishing for the extracts on pp. 57 and the revision exercise no 5 p. 39 in the Teacher's Book from *Urban Myths Unplugged* by Phil Healey and Rick Granvill; *The Economist* for the text on p. 59 © *The Economist*, London 1994 and the magazine's logo on p. 72; *The Financial Times* for the article on p. 61 © *The Financial Times* 1994; Express Newspapers plc for the headline 'How museums are turning us into fossils' on p. 64 from *The Daily Express* 1996; British Sky Broadcasting Ltd for the *Sky News* logo on p. 61; *The Guardian* for the headline 'Pizzas on Antarctic trek' on p. 64 © *The Guardian*; *Private Eye* for the text on p. 70 from 'Great Bores of Today', November 1995; The National Magazine Company Ltd for the *Cosmopolitan*, *Country Living* and *She* logos on p. 72; *Reader's Digest*, *Literary Review*, and *Hello!* for their logos on p. 72; *Bella* for the article on p. 73; Cassell plc for the text on p. 82 from *Play the Game: Table Tennis* by Donald Parker and David Hewitt, published by Blandford; Dorling Kindersley for the text on p. 91 from *Learn to Video in a Week-end* by Roland Lewis; Wayland Publishers Ltd for the illustrations on p. 104 and the story 'Six Dinner Sid' on p. 105 and on the cassette by Inga Moore; The poem 'The Lion' on p. 106 and on the cassette is from *Dirty Beasts* by Roald Dahl published by Jonathan Cape; The Pierpont Morgan Library, New York (MA 2696) for the letter by Charlotte Brontë on p. 117; Harvard University Press for the letter on p. 118 from *Letters of Robert Browning and Elizabeth Barrett Browning*, edited by Elvan Kinter, Cambridge Mass.: Copyright © 1969 by President and Fellows of Harvard College, reprinted by permission of Harvard University Press; Sheil Land Associates Ltd for the texts on pp. 120 from *The Sunday Times punctuation made easy in one hour* by Graham King, © 1994 and the revision exercise no 6 p. 151 in the Teacher's Book from *The Sunday Times crisp clear punctuation in one hour* by

Graham King © 1993, both published by Mandarin; *Time* magazine for the article on p. 129 by Christine Gorman; Stephen Applebaum for the reviews on *Shoot the Pianist* on p. 130, *The Color Purple* and *Aladdin* on p. 131; Video World for the reviews on *Jurassic Park* and *The House of the Spirits* on p. 131; Pan Books for the book cover of *High Stakes* by Dick Francis on p. 136; The Orion Publishing Group Ltd for the book cover of *Persuasion* by Jane Austen on p. 136; Deborah Cameron for the extract from her lecture 'Verbal Hygiene for Women: Linguistics Misapplied' on the cassette (Unit 20); *The New Scientist* for the text on p. 144 by Rosie Mestel; The text on p. 148 is reprinted by permission of Fourth Estate Ltd and Regina Ryan Publishing Enterprises, Inc., 251 Central Park West, New York, New York 10024, USA from *Look Yourself Up* by Bernard Ashbell and Karen Wynn. © 1991 by Bernard Ashbell and Regina Ryan Publishing Enterprises, Inc. © 1992 by Bernard Ashbell and Karen Wynn; Penguin Books Ltd and David Inshow for the book cover of *Modern British Short Stories*, Penguin Books Ltd for the book cover of *Tales of the Unexpected* by Roald Dahl and Arrow Books Ltd for the book cover of *Victoria Line Central Line* by Maeve Binchy on p. 149; Reed Consumer Books Ltd for the extracts from *Benefactors* by Michael Frayn from *Plays: Two*, published by Methuen London on pp. 155-157 and on the cassette; Michael Imison Playwrights Ltd for the extract on the cassette (Unit 24) from 'Yes, Prime Minister' © 1986 by Anthony Jay and Jonathan Lynn. By permission of Michael Imison Playwrights Ltd, 28 Almeida Street, London, N1 1TD; *The Sun* for the newspaper's front page on p. 166, reproduced by kind permission of *The Sun*; BMJ Publishing Group for the journal's cover on p. 166; the poems on p. 167 and the revision exercises no 7 p. 151 and no 7 p. 153 are extracts from 'On and on and on' and 'And on and on' from *Lucky* by Roger McGough published by Puffin Books, 1994, reprinted by permission of the Peters Fraser and Dunlop Group Limited on behalf of Roger McGough; The Estate of F. Scott Fitzgerald for the letter in the revision exercise no 5 p. 118 in the Teacher's Book, reprinted by permission of Harold Ober Associates Incorporate. Copyright © 1963 by Frances S. F. Lanahan; renewed 1991; the phonetic symbols on p.175 are reproduced from *Cambridge International Dictionary of English* © Cambridge University Press.

The publishers and author are grateful to the following illustrators and photographic sources:

Illustrators: Rowan Barnes-Murphy: pp. 41, 79, 103, 150; Kathy Baxendale: pp. 8, 48, 82; Ken Brooks: p. 167; Chris Burke: pp. 31, 70, 71, 96, 123, 146; Philip Emms: pp. 27, 60, 99, 128; Martin Fish: pp. 25, 40, 53, 67, 98, 106, 160, 161; Maggie Ling: pp. 29, 69, 95, 132, 133; Inga Moore: p. 104; Mark Peppé: pp. 7, 116; Sue Shields: pp. 23, 50, 86, 159; Katherine Walker: pp. 21, 39, 46, 51, 92, 93, 121, 134, 135; Bob Wilson: pp. 15, 34, 35, 57, 84, 85, 142, 151; Annabel Wright: pp. 42, 87, 100, 127.

Photographic sources: Action Plus: p. 88 *mr, br*; Allsport (U.K.) Ltd: pp. 81 *cricket, horse racing, baseball, snooker*, 82, 88 *tr, bl*; The Bridgeman Art Library Ltd: p. 117 *t*; The Cambridgeshire Collection, Cambridge Central Library: pp. 156, 157; Collections: pp. 73 *b*, 75 *tc*, 108, 154 *t*; Mary Evans Picture Library Ltd: pp. 117 *b*, 118, 120; The Ronald Grant Archive: pp. 30, 130 *br*, 131 *br*; The Robert Harding Picture Library: p.124; The Hulton Getty Picture Collection Ltd: pp. 73 *t*, 111, 114; Images Colour Library Ltd: pp. 9 *br*, 36 *bl*, 61 *b*, 97 *tl*, 125 *tr, ml*, 154 *m*; The Image Bank: pp. 33 *t*, 36 *tl, mc*, 75 *br*, 81 *cycling, football*, 97 *tc, tr, bl, bc*, 125 *tl*; Impact Photos Ltd: p. 94; The Kobal Collection Ltd: pp. 129, 130 *bl*, 131 *tl, tr*; Bryan Ledgard: p. 37 *tl*; Jerry Mason/Science Photo Library Ltd: p. 44 *m*; Performing Arts Library: p. 9 *ml*; Pictor International Ltd: pp. 75 *mc*, 125 *mr*; Philipe Plailly/Eurelios/Science Photo Library Ltd: p. 44 *b*; Pictor International: pp. 9 *tr*, 55 *t*; Popperfoto: pp. 12, 16, 154 *b*; Redferns: pp. 37 *tr*, 41 *ml, bl, bc, br*; Rex Features Ltd: pp. 41 *mr*, 44 *t*, 75 *tl*, 144, 163; Frank Spooner Pictures Ltd: p.143; Tony Stone Images: pp. 9 *bl*, 33 *ml, mr, b*, 36 *tr, mr*, 58 *bl, br*, 61 *m*, 63, 65, 75 *ml*, 81 *motor racing, tennis, swimming, table tennis, golf, hockey*, 88 *tl*, 91 *r*, 97 *br*, 102, 106, 125 *tc, mc*, 137, 147; Sygma Ltd: p. 13; John Walmsley Photo-Library: p. 75 *bl*.

Commissioned photography: Jeremy Pembrey: pp. 6, 36 *br*, 58 *m*, 68, 75 *tr*, *bc*, 88 *ml*, 90, 110, 113, 158.

t = top, *m* = middle, *b* = bottom, *c* – centre, *r* = right

Picture research by Mandy Twells

Design and composition by Newton Harris